Easy Microsoft® Word 97

Sherry Kinkoph

D0731210

Easy Microsoft® Word 97

Library of Congress Catalog Card Number: 0-7897-1024-2

International Standard Book Number: 96-71449

98 97   8   7   6   5   4   3   2

Interpretation of the printing code: the rightmost double-digit number is the year of the book's first printing; the rightmost single-digit number is the number of the book's printing. For example, a printing code of 96-1 shows that this copy of the book was printed during the first printing of the book in 1996.

Screen reproductions in this book were created by means of the program Collage Complete from Inner Media, Inc, Hollis, NH.

Printed in the United States of America

Dedication

To the Daniel's family: Tina, Tim, Andrew, Teal, and future author Teisha.

Credits

Publisher
Roland Elgey

Publishing Manager
Lynn E. Zingraf

Editorial Services Director
Elizabeth Keaffaber

Managing Editor
Michael Cunningham

Director of Marketing
Lynn E. Zingraf

Acquisitions Editor
Martha O'Sullivan

Technical Support Specialist
Nadeem Muhammed

Technical Specialist
Herbert C. Feltner

Product Development Specialist
Lisa Bucki

Technical Editor
Ed Hanley

Production Editor
Katie Purdum

Book Designers
Barbara Kordesh
Ruth Harvey

Cover Designers
Dan Armstrong
Kim Scott

Production Team
Tammy Ahrens
Toi Davis
Sean Decker
Stephanie Hammett
Deb Kincaid
Holly Wittenberg

Indexer
Craig A. Small

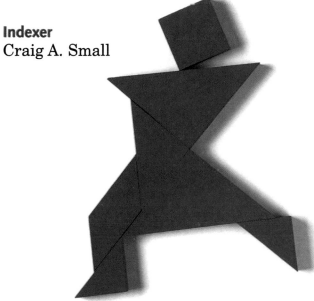

Composed in *Syntax* and *New Century Schoolbook* by Que Corporation

We'd Like to Hear from You!

As part of our continuing effort to produce books of the highest possible quality, Que would like to hear your comments. To stay competitive, we *really* want you, as a computer book reader and user, to let us know what you like or dislike most about this book or other Que products.

You can mail comments, ideas, or suggestions for improving future editions to the address below, or send us a fax at (317) 581-4663. For the online inclined, Macmillan Computer Publishing has a forum on CompuServe (type **GO QUEBOOKS** at any prompt) through which our staff and authors are available for questions and comments. The address of our Internet site is **http://www.mcp.com/que** (World Wide Web).

In addition to exploring our forum, please feel free to contact me personally to discuss your opinions of this book: I'm **75703,3251** on CompuServe, and I'm **lgentry@que.mcp.com** on the Internet.

Although we cannot provide general technical support, we're happy to help you resolve problems you encounter related to our books, disks, or other products. If you need such assistance, please contact our Tech Support department at **800-545-5914 ext. 3833.**

To order other Que or Macmillan Computer Publishing books or products, please call our Customer Service department at **800-835-3202 ext. 666.**

Thanks in advance—your comments will help us to continue publishing the best books available on computer topics in today's market.

Lorna Gentry
Senior Product Development Specialist
Que Corporation
201 W. 103rd Street
Indianapolis, Indiana 46290
USA

About the Author

Sherry Kinkoph has authored many computer books for Macmillan Publishing over the past five years, including books for both adults and children. Her recent publications include *The Complete Idiot's Guide to Microsoft Office for Windows 95, The 10 Minute Guide to Schedule+ for Windows 95, The 10 Minute Guide to Lotus Organizer 97,* and *The Big Basics Book of Microsoft Office for Windows 95.*

Sherry started exploring computers back in college, and claims that many term papers were "whipped out" using a trustworthy 128K Macintosh. Today, Sherry's still churning out words, but now they're in the form of books. Instead of using a Mac, she's moved on to a PC. A native of the Midwest, Sherry currently resides in Fishers, IN and continues her quest to help beginning users master the ever-changing computer technologies.

Acknowledgments

Special thanks to everyone who helped contribute directly to the creation of this book: Martha O'Sullivan, Lisa Bucki, Katie Purdum, and the crew in Production.

Trademarks

Contents

Part III: Managing Word 97 Files — 69

Part IV: Formatting Your Document — 93

Part V: More Editing Techniques — 121

Part VI: More Formatting — 141

Contents

Part X: Sample Documents   223

Index   240

Introduction

Welcome to Easy Word 97, a book designed and created specifically for beginner users. If you're new to the world of computers and to the Word 97 program, this book is just for you. You'll learn how to use Word 97 by following easy step-by-step tasks, without all the technical gobbledy-gook associated with most computer manuals. You'll learn all about the basics you need to successfully use Word 97 to create documents of your own.

What You Can Do with Word 97

One of the most popular word processing programs in use today, Microsoft Word is a tool for creating all kinds of documents using your computer. Microsoft Word has been around for awhile, and just keeps getting better and better with each new edition of the program. In this book, we'll cover Word 97.

Word 97 is a program designed specifically for creating letters, reports, research papers, memos, flyers, and any other types of documents you can think of. With Word, you can easily make changes to the documents you create before you print them out. You can also add tables, pictures, and other items to make your documents more interesting.

Here are some other functions you can perform with Word 97:

- *Correct mistakes.*   It's easy to fix errors with Word 97—and you don't need a bottle of White-Out. You can correct a mistake on-screen when you see it, long before you print the document.

- *Move around quickly.*   You can quickly navigate a document on-screen with a click of the mouse button. You can zip from one paragraph to another, or from page to page. You can even move from the top of the document to the bottom without a pause.

- *Make editing changes.*   With Word 97, you can insert text into any location in your document. You can also quickly delete text, whether it's one character or a whole block of text.

- *Rearrange your text.*   If you create a document and then change your mind about the order of the text, you can easily move and copy text from one location to another.

- *Restore deleted text.* If you accidentally delete text that you want to keep, you don't have to worry about retyping it back in again. Instead, you can just restore the text with Word's Undo commands.

- *Check spelling.* If you're not the best speller in the world, Word's AutoCorrect feature can really help you out. As you type, Word's spelling features check your words for misspellings and double words.

- *Search for text.* Need to find out how many times you used the word "success" in a document? Want to locate the paragraph where you talk about future goals? You can quickly search your entire document for a particular word or phrase.

- *Search and replace text.* Just as you can quickly locate words and phrases in your document, you can also make text replacements. For example, you can change all occurrences of the name Smith to Smythe.

- *Make formatting changes.* Word 97 enables you to change margins, tabs, and other formatting options easily. You can experiment with the settings until the document appears the way that you want it. Then, you can print it.

- *Change how your text looks when you print it.* With Word 97, you can turn ordinary type into bold, italicized, or underlined text to make it really stand out. Also, depending on your printer, you can change typefaces to create a different look.

- *Preview your document.* You can preview your document to see how it will look when you print it. The preview feature saves you time and wasted paper.

- *Add bulleted lists.* Add bullets to your document to emphasize text. Word 97 has supplied a range of bullets depending upon your preference or needs. You can also easily add numbered lists to your documents.

- *Add borders.* Borders can be added to any text, paragraph, or an entire document. They can be created in a variety of widths—from thin to thick. There's even a 3-D effect available for creating special effects.

- *Create headers and footers.* Word offers the capability to create custom headers and footers for your documents, or you can choose from the standard selections that are offered.

- *Import data or graphics into your document.* You're not just limited to items you create within Word 97. You can import pictures or data from other applications into your documents.

- *Create standardized documents.* If you're ever at a loss about the type of documents you want to make, you can use Word's templates and wizards to create standardized and customized documents.

As you can see from this list, Word 97 has a lot of features you can use to create documents of all kinds, and you'll learn how to apply these features, as well as others, using this book.

Task Sections

You'll find 10 Parts in this book, and each covers a particular aspect of the Word 97 program, as explained in this list:

- Part I helps you get acquainted with the Word 97 program and includes tasks for opening and closing the program, using the on-screen elements, and finding online help.

- In Part II, you'll learn the basics of entering data into a Word document, including copying, moving, and deleting data.

- Part III gives you the basics for managing your Word 97 files. You'll learn how to save and close files, and how to create new ones based on templates.

- Part IV shows you how to add formatting to change the way your text looks. You'll learn how to make text bold, how to change text alignment, how to create bulleted lists, and more.

- In Part V you'll learn important editing techniques for searching through documents, checking spelling, and even using an electronic thesaurus.

- Part VI offers more formatting techniques you can use to control how your documents look.

- Part VII shows you how to enhance your documents with graphics, shapes, tables, and color.

- In Part VIII you will learn how to preview and print Word documents. You'll also learn about Word's various screen views and zooming features.

- Part IX gives you tasks for communicating with others using Word 97. You'll learn how to create a form letter and envelopes, turn your documents into e-mail messages, and design your own Web page to post on the Internet.

- Finally, Part X lets you see some sample documents created with Word 97, utilizing many of the features covered in the book.

Introduction

The tasks in each part of this book include numbered steps that tell you how to accomplish certain activities, such as saving a document or indenting a paragraph. The numbered steps walk you through a specific example so that you can learn the task by actually doing it.

Big Screen

At the beginning of each task is a large screen that shows how the computer screen will look at some key point in the task. Sometimes, this will show what the screen looks like when you are finished. Other times, it will be an important step along the way.

19

Going to a Specific Page

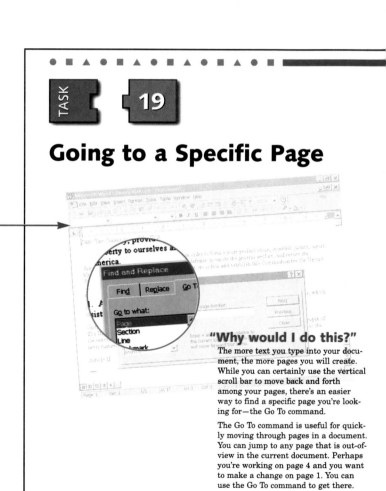

"Why would I do this?"

The more text you type into your document, the more pages you will create. While you can certainly use the vertical scroll bar to move back and forth among your pages, there's an easier way to find a specific page you're looking for—the Go To command.

The Go To command is useful for quickly moving through pages in a document. You can jump to any page that is out-of-view in the current document. Perhaps you're working on page 4 and you want to make a change on page 1. You can use the Go To command to get there.

Step-by-Step Screens

Each task includes a screen shot for each numbered step of a procedure. The screen shot shows how the computer screen looks at each step in the process.

Task 19: Going to a Specific Page

1 Open the **Edit** menu and select **Go To**. This selects the Go To command.

Missing Link

Notice that the Go To tab has other elements you can go to besides document pages. You can also use this tab to locate footnotes, sections, and more.

Missing Link Tips

Many tasks include Missing Link tip boxes that tell you a little more about a procedure or alert you to a time-saving shortcut.

Puzzled Tips

You may find that you performed a task, such as italicizing text by following the numbered steps, but that the results don't turn out the way you expected. The Puzzled tip boxes tell you what common problems you may expect or how to proceed if something doesn't work as planned.

2 Word 97 opens the Find and Replace dialog box, with the Go To tab at the front of the dialog box. (If the Go To tab isn't at the front, just click on the **Go To** tab name.)

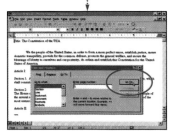

3 Click inside the **Enter page number** text box and type in the page number you want to turn to, then click on the **Go To** command button. Word 97 displays the page you specified. Click the **Close** button to close the dialog box. ■

Puzzled?

If you mistakenly moved to the wrong page, repeat the Go To command, but type the correct page number to move to the page you want.

PART I

Acquaint Yourself with the Word Screen

W HEN IT COMES TO WORD PROCESSING PROGRAMS, Microsoft Word is the top-selling application of its kind. You can use it to create professional-looking letters, reports, tables, memos, flyers, and much more. You can create almost anything that involves text using Word.

You can buy Word 97 for Windows 95 as a stand-alone product or as part of a suite of programs called Microsoft Office 97. Office 97 contains Word, plus several other programs that complement one another, such as a spreadsheet and a presentation graphics program. Regardless of whether you're using Word 97 by itself or with the Office 97 suite, this book can help you get up and running fast.

Part I of this book will acquaint you with the Microsoft Word 97 program, including tasks that focus on navigating the Word 97 window. You'll learn how to start and exit Word, how to use the toolbars, and how to find help when you need it.

The Word 97 screen has several features to learn about, as described in the following table:

If you're using Microsoft's IntelliMouse (a new mouse from Microsoft that may have come with your Office 97 program package), which has a wheel button, there are some additional mouse movements you can perform:

Wheel forward and *wheel backward* are movements used to move up and down a scroll bar. The IntelliMouse's wheel button lets you scroll without having to click on a scroll bar arrow or drag a scroll box.

Panning is when you hold down the wheel button and move the mouse. Panning lets you scroll around an entire document in any direction without using the scroll bars.

Zooming is when you press the **Ctrl** key and hold down the wheel button. The zooming feature lets you zoom your view of a document to see text up close or far away.

Screen Elements

Screen Element	Description
Title bar	The bar at the very top of the screen that lists the program and file name.
Menu bar	The next bar down contains a list of menu names you can use to display and select commands.
Standard toolbar	A bar with icons you can click on to activate commonly-used commands.
Formatting toolbar	Another bar of icons and drop-down lists you can use to format your document's text.
Ruler	Use to set margins and tabs for your document.
Insertion point	A flashing vertical line that appears in the document window, marking where the text you type is inserted.
Scroll bars	Use the vertical bar at the right of your screen, and the horizontal bar near the bottom of the screen to move around in your document.
Status bar	The bottom bar on the screen displays information about the document you're working on.

If you're ever in a jam, you can get instant help with Word 97's help features, including a Help index and the Answer Wizard. Word even offers you a tip of the day, featuring tips and tricks for numerous Word operations.

The tasks in this part teach you the skills you'll need to perform many of Word 97's basic operations.

Starting and Exiting Word 97

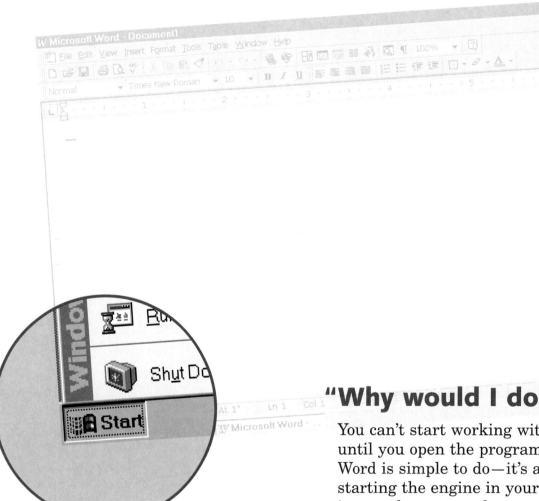

"Why would I do this?"

You can't start working with Word 97 until you open the program. Starting Word is simple to do—it's as easy as starting the engine in your car! Assuming you have turned on your computer and monitor, Windows 95 appears on your screen. Let's jump right in and start Word 97 now. (When you're done working in Word, you can exit Word and return to the Windows 95 desktop.)

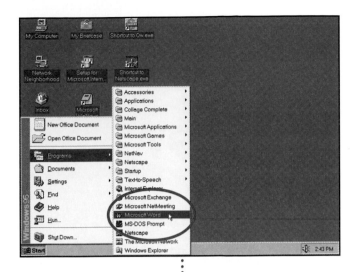

1 Open the **Start** menu, select **Programs**, and **Microsoft Word**.

Puzzled?

When you use the mouse to execute a command, make sure you point and click the left mouse button. If nothing happens, or if a strange menu appears, check the location of the mouse pointer and try clicking again.

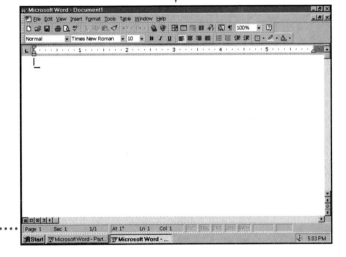

2 The Word 97 start-up screen appears, then a blank document opens onto your screen. Welcome to Word 97.

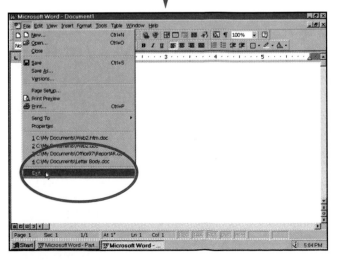

3 To close the program at any time, pull down the **File** menu and select **Exit**. This step ends your Microsoft Word session and closes the program. You return to the Windows desktop. ■

Puzzled?

When exiting the program, Word prompts you to save your document if you've made any changes. If you don't want to save your changes, click the **No** button. (Learn about saving files in Task 20 in Part III.)

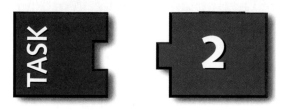

TASK 2

Working with Word 97 Windows

"Why would I do this?"

When you open the Word 97 program, it appears as a window on your screen. Within the window are tools and other on-screen elements to help you use the program, among which are several buttons for controlling the program window itself—the Minimize, Maximize, and Close buttons. You'll find all three of these buttons in the upper-right corner of the window.

You can use these buttons to change how the program window appears on your screen. You may want to reduce the size of the window so you can see other items on the Windows 95 desktop. Or perhaps you'll want to minimize the window completely so that it appears as a button on the Windows 95 taskbar.

The document window's Minimize, Maximize, and Close buttons are located on the far right side of the menu bar. You can minimize the document window and open a new document window to type in, or you can close a document window without closing the entire Word 97 program.

It's a good idea to spend a few minutes mastering the window controls. Once you learn these controls, you can apply the same techniques when you work with other program windows.

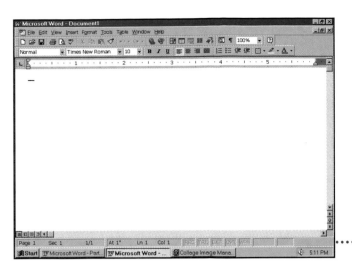

1 Open the Word 97 program window, if it isn't open already. If you need help with this step, see Task 1, "Starting and Exiting Word 97."

2 Click on the **Minimize** button (the button with the minus sign) in the upper right corner of the program window. This reduces the Word 97 window into a button on the Windows 95 taskbar at the bottom of the screen.

> **Missing Link**
>
> To close the application window and exit Word 97 entirely, click the **Close** (**X**) button in the upper right corner of the application window.

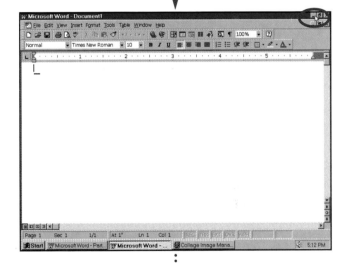

3 To return the Word 97 window to its original size, click the **Microsoft Word** button on the taskbar at the bottom of the Windows 95 desktop.

15

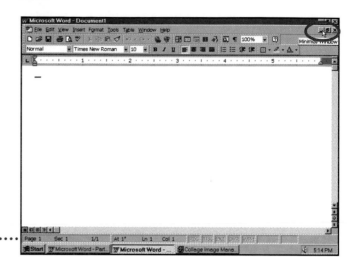

4 Now let's work with the document window's controls. Click the document window's **Minimize** button near the right end of the menu bar. The document will then appear as a button above the Windows taskbar.

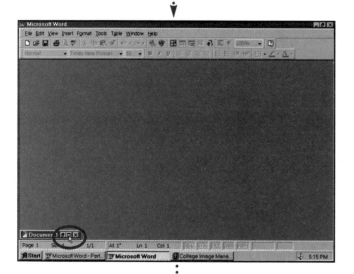

5 To enlarge the document window again, click the **Maximize** icon (it looks like a full-size window) on the document button. Word enlarges the document window to full size.

> **Missing Link**
>
> To restore the application or document window to its previous size, click the application or document window's **Restore** button (the icon that looks like two overlapping windows).

6 To completely close the document, click the **Close** (**X**) button in the upper-right corner of the document window. Word closes the document window, leaving an empty gray area on your Word 97 screen. ■

> **Missing Link**
>
> To open a new document window, click on the **New** button on the Standard toolbar or open the **File** menu and select **New**.

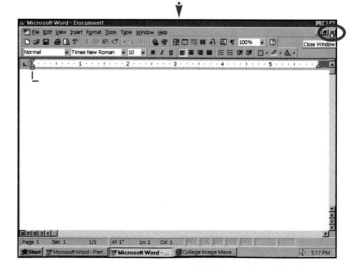

Selecting a Menu Command

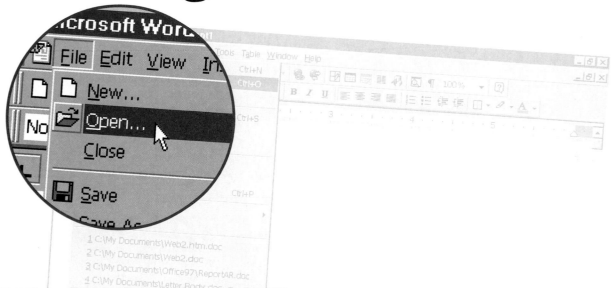

"Why would I do this?"

The menu bar contains lists of commands you can use to execute Word tasks. Located directly below the Word 97 title bar (the bar at the very top of the Word screen), the menu bar consists of nine pull-down menus to select from (although menu names may change depending on the task you're working on).

To display a menu, you simply click on the menu name. When the menu is displayed, you'll see a list of commands related to the menu topic. For example, if you want to open a new document file, you can display the File menu and find the New command.

When it comes to selecting menu commands, it's as easy as choosing from a

real menu. Simply click on the command you want to activate. Some menu commands you select may display additional menu lists to choose from. Menu commands followed by an ellipses (...) indicate that a dialog box or another window will appear after you select the command (turn to Task 5, "Working with Dialog Boxes" to learn more). Text combinations, such as Ctrl+C, listed to the right of a command are shortcut keys. Shortcut keys are keys you can press from the keyboard to activate the command.

Let's practice opening a menu and selecting a command.

Task 3: Selecting a Menu Command

1 Point to the word **File** in the menu bar, then click the left mouse button. This step opens the menu. In this case, you're opening the File menu and displaying a list of File commands.

Missing Link

Many of the commands found in Word 97's menu lists can also be activated by clicking on a toolbar icon. Learn more about using the toolbars in Task 6, "Working with the Toolbars."

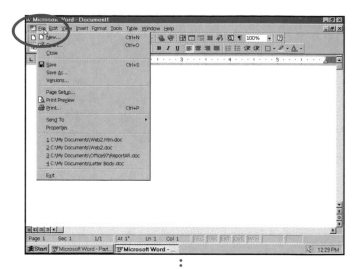

2 Now select a menu command. Point to **Open** and click the left mouse button. The Open dialog box appears.

Missing Link

The icons that you see next to some menu commands match the icons found on Word 97's toolbars. Pay attention to the icons associated with each menu command so you can learn to recognize them on the toolbars. It's easier to click on a toolbar button than it is to open a menu and select a command.

3 Click on the **Close** button in the upper right corner of the dialog box, or click the **Cancel** button to close the Open dialog box. ■

Missing Link

To close a menu without making a selection, click anywhere else on the screen, outside of the menu or press **Esc** from the keyboard.

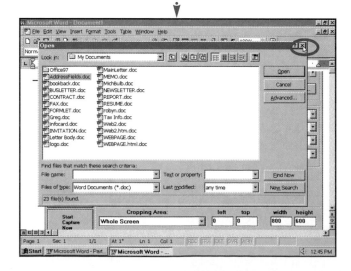

Using Shortcut Menus

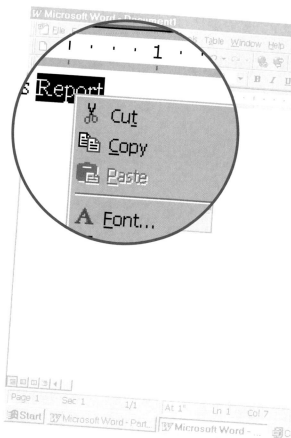

"Why would I do this?"

Another type of menu you can use with Word 97 is a shortcut menu. A shortcut menu pops up on your screen when you click the right mouse button. For example, if you're in the middle of entering text and you decide you want to change the formatting to make the text stand out, you can use a shortcut menu to help you. Simply right-click to display a shortcut menu and select the appropriate formatting command you want to apply.

Shortcut menus include commands you can use to quickly edit or format text or cells. Those same commands are readily available from the menu bar or the toolbars, but it's often just as easy to right-click and display an instant menu to choose from.

Now let's take a look at a shortcut menu that contains editing and formatting commands and learn how to use it.

Task 4: Using Shortcut Menus

1 Type in some text, such as the words **Sales Report**. This enters text into the blank Word 97 document. This is the text you will change using the shortcut menu.

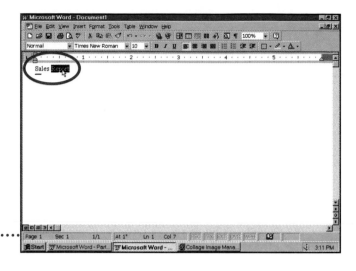

2 Point to the text you just typed and click the right mouse button. This opens a shortcut menu displaying a list of editing and formatting commands.

> **Puzzled?**
>
> Sometimes, you'll display a shortcut menu that doesn't have the command you want. To leave a shortcut menu without making a selection, click outside the shortcut menu or press the **Esc** key.

3 Click on **Bullets and Numbering** from the shortcut menu. This opens the Bullets and Numbering dialog box from which you can add bullets to your text or create a numbered list. Click on the **Cancel** button to close the dialog box without making any changes. ∎

> **Puzzled?**
>
> To delete the text you typed in for this task, click the mouse pointer directly at the end of the words "Sales Report," and press the **Backspace** key until all the text is deleted.

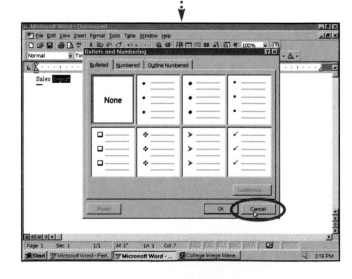

Working with Dialog Boxes

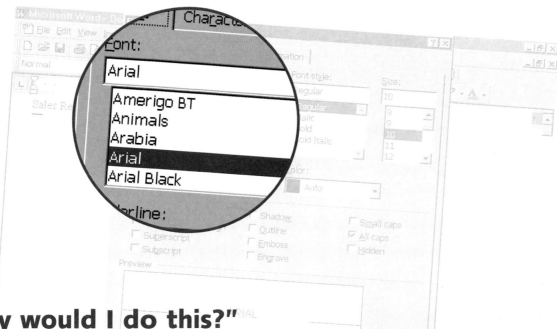

"Why would I do this?"

Many of the Word commands you select result in a dialog box appearing on-screen. Dialog boxes are another way in which the program communicates with you. Some dialog boxes prompt you for additional information, others might confirm information or warn you about a task you're about to perform. The most common dialog boxes are the ones that let you select additional options.

When you select a menu command followed by (...), Word displays a dialog box containing options you can choose. For example, when you open the **Format** menu and select **Font**, the

Font dialog box appears. The Font dialog box contains all kinds of options for controlling the appearance of text, such as font styles, sizes, and color. You simply make your selections, then click **OK** to exit the box and apply the options you chose.

Many of the dialog boxes you run across using Word 97 contain one or more of the following elements: tabs, list boxes, drop-down lists, text boxes, check boxes, option buttons, and command buttons. Let's examine a dialog box and find out how to use its elements.

21

Task 5: Working with Dialog Boxes

1 Open the **Format** menu and select **Font**. This opens the Font dialog box.

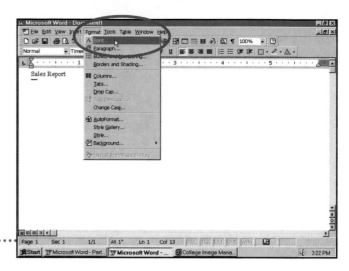

2 The Font dialog box has several list boxes. Click the up or down scroll arrow at the right side of the **Font** list box to scroll through the list of fonts. To select a font, click the font name in the list. The name of the font you select appears in the text box above the list box and an example of the font appears in the Preview box. In the figure, Arial is the selected font.

3 Now let's select an item in a drop-down list. Click the down arrow next to the **Underline** box. You see a list of underline styles. Click an underline style to select it. For example, the (None) style is selected in the figure.

Puzzled?

Sometimes a drop-down list doesn't have the item you want. To leave a drop-down list without making a selection, click anywhere outside it.

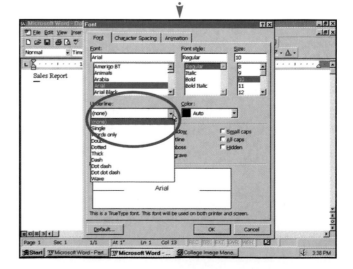

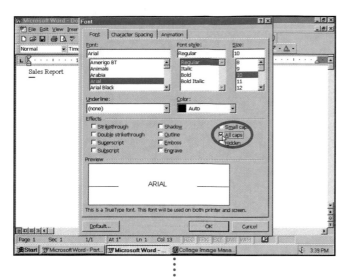

4 Check boxes and option buttons are used to turn features on or off. Click a check box to select an option in the **Effects** area, such as the **All Caps** option selected in the figure. A check mark appears in the check box, indicating that you selected the option.

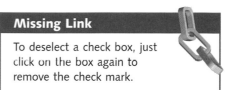

Missing Link

To deselect a check box, just click on the box again to remove the check mark.

5 Some dialog boxes have a lot of options to choose from and use tabs (which look like actual folder tabs) to keep the information organized. Click a tab to bring another set of options to the front of the dialog box. For example, click on **the Character Spacing** tab in the Font dialog box to display the character spacing options.

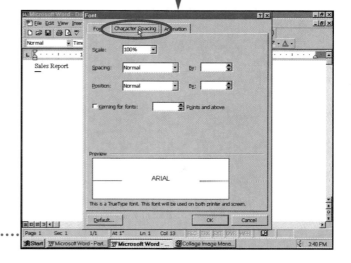

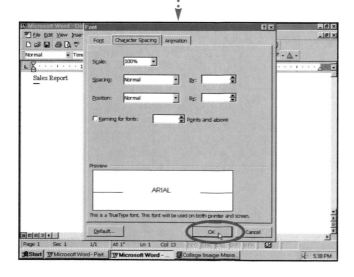

6 When you're finally ready to apply the options you selected in the dialog box, click the **OK** command button. Command buttons are used to activate the selections, or to cancel and exit the dialog box. Some command buttons, when selected, open additional dialog boxes containing more options to choose from. To exit the Font dialog box or any other one without making any changes, click on the **Cancel** button. ■

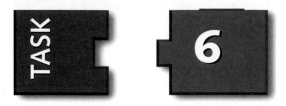

Working with the Toolbars

"Why would I do this?"

If you're looking for a faster, easier way to carry out commands, toolbars are the answer. Word's toolbars are loaded with icon buttons you can click to quickly activate commonly-used commands. Instead of pulling down a menu and selecting a command, you can easily point and click at toolbar icons to carry out many of the same tasks found on the menus.

There are lots of toolbars in Word 97, thirteen in all. Depending on what task you're trying to complete, your screen may show different toolbars. By default, Word 97 displays the Standard and Formatting toolbars, which happen to be the two most commonly used tool-

bars. The Standard toolbar (located directly beneath the menu bar) contains common editing buttons, and the Formatting toolbar (beneath the Standard toolbar) contains icons and drop-down lists that help you format text quickly.

However, you can hide or display the various toolbars as needed. For example, if you need more room on-screen to see the document you're working on, you can hide the Standard and Formatting toolbars.

In this task, you'll learn how to select a toolbar icon and how to hide a toolbar like the Standard toolbar.

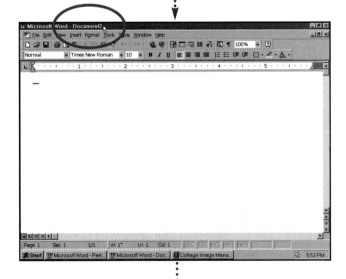

1 If you ever want to know what a particular toolbar button does, check out the ScreenTip feature. Simply point to the toolbar icon and pause. The button's name appears next to the icon. This is the ScreenTip feature.

Puzzled?

Be sure to move the mouse pointer directly over the toolbar icon in order to view the button's name. If the ScreenTip does not appear, try moving the mouse pointer again and pause a few seconds.

2 To select a toolbar button, just click on the icon. For example, click the **New** icon. Word opens a new document (notice DOCUMENT2 now appears on top of DOCUMENT1).

3 To close an open document (the new document, in this case), open the **File** menu and select **Close**. Word closes the DOCUMENT2 document. DOCUMENT1 is now the active document again.

Task 6: Working with the Toolbars

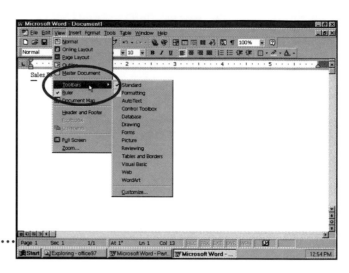

4 To hide a toolbar, using the Standard toolbar as an example, first open the **View** menu and select the **Toolbars** command. This displays another menu listing the Word 97 toolbars. A check mark next to the toolbar name indicates that a toolbar is displayed.

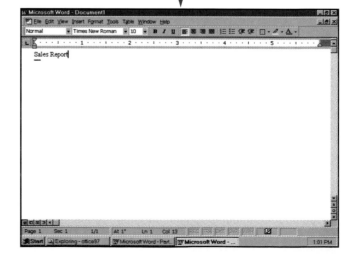

5 Click on **Standard**. This removes the check mark and instructs Word to hide the Standard toolbar.

6 As you can see in the figure, the Standard toolbar is now hidden. To display the Standard toolbar again, open the **View** menu, select **Toolbars**, and select **Standard**. ■

Hiding the Ruler

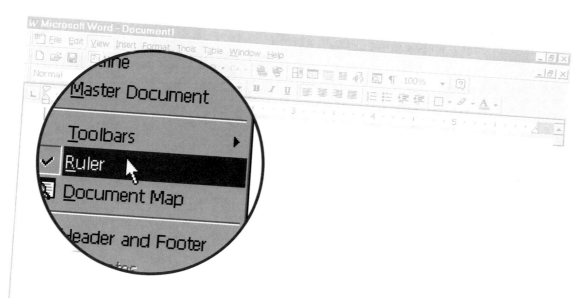

"Why would I do this?"

By default, the ruler appears directly beneath the Formatting toolbar. You can use the ruler to quickly change tabs and margins (which you'll learn how to do in Part IV of this book). However, you might want to hide the ruler so you can see more of the document you're working on, or perhaps the ruler is distracting and you'd like a cleaner-looking screen. You can easily hide the ruler and display it again when you want to use it.

In this task, you'll learn how to hide the ruler.

Task 7: Hiding the Ruler

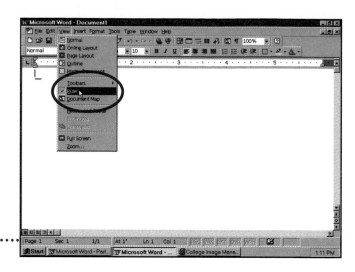

1 Open the **View** menu. You see a list of View commands. Notice that a check mark appears next to the Ruler command on the menu, which indicates that you have the Ruler displayed.

2 Click on **Ruler** to remove the check mark next to it. The menu disappears, and the ruler is now hidden.

3 To display the ruler again, open the **View** menu, then select **Ruler**. ■

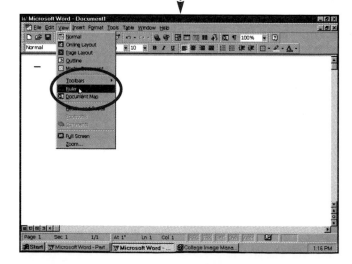

TASK 8

Getting Help

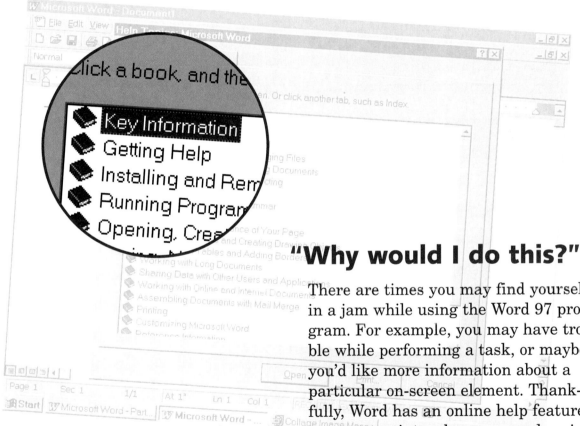

"Why would I do this?"

There are times you may find yourself in a jam while using the Word 97 program. For example, you may have trouble while performing a task, or maybe you'd like more information about a particular on-screen element. Thankfully, Word has an online help feature you can tap into when you need assistance.

You can consult a help index and contents, find tips for using the certain elements of the program, and look up step-by-step explanations while you work.

In the steps to follow, you'll learn how to access several of Word's help features.

Task 8: Getting Help

1 Open the **Help** menu and choose **Contents and Index**. This tells Word to open the Help Topics window and you see a list of Help topics arranged by category. Each category icon looks like a tiny book.

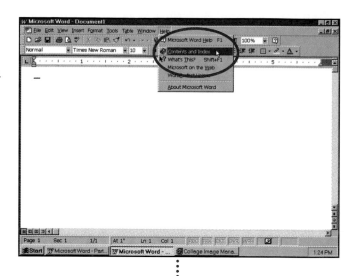

Missing Link

To open Help to the appropriate topic for what you're working on, you can press **F1**. You can also click the **What's This** button (?) in the upper right corner of a dialog box to get help on the command for which you are setting options.

2 Double-click the category icon for **Opening, Creating and Saving Documents**. A sublist of topics appears beneath the selected category.

3 Double-click the category icon for **Opening Documents**. A sublist of specific topics pertaining to creating and opening documents appears.

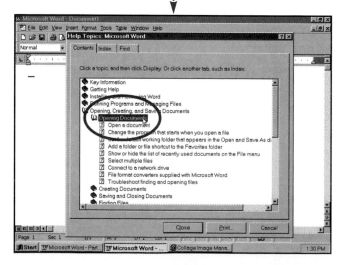

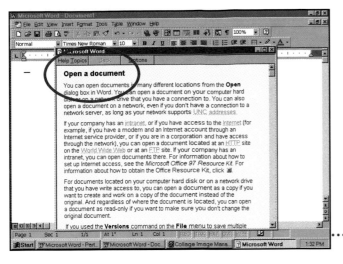

4 To view information about a specific topic, double-click the topic icon. For our example, double-click on **Open a document**. This step opens the Microsoft Word help window and displays information or the steps about opening a document.

5 When finished viewing the information, you can close the Help window by clicking the **Close** button located in the upper right corner of the Help window.

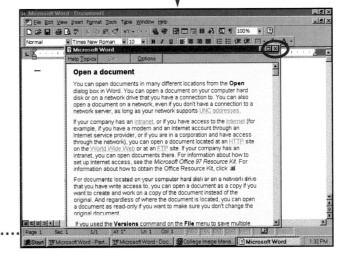

6 Another type of help you can summon in Word is the What's This feature. Open the **Help** menu again, and this time select **What's This**.

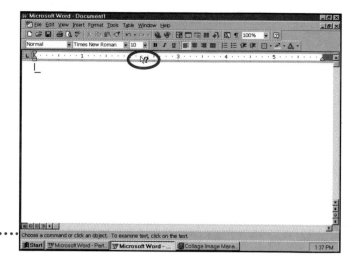

7 The mouse pointer on your screen now takes the shape of a pointer with a question mark. Point at any area of the screen you want to learn more about, such as the ruler, then click the left mouse button.

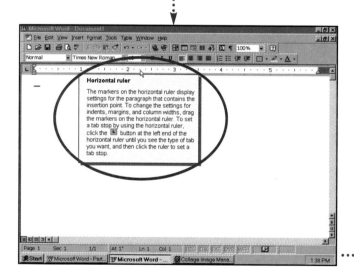

8 Word 97 displays a What's This box offering more details about the on-screen item or task you're trying to perform. After you read the information, click anywhere outside the box, or press **Esc**.

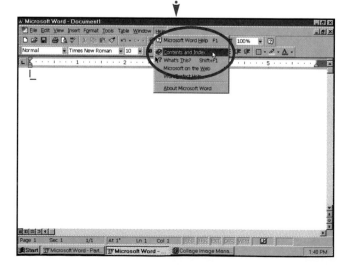

9 If you prefer to look up things yourself, you can use Word's Help index. Open the **Help** menu again and select **Contents and Index**. This opens the Help Topics box again.

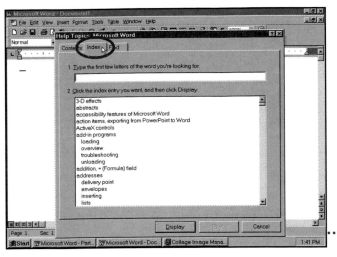

10 If the Index tab isn't at the front of the dialog box, click on the **Index** tab. The Index tab has an alphabetized index of help topics you can look up. You simply type in the word or words you want to find and the index turns right to the topic you're looking for.

11 To look up a help topic, type in the first few letters of the term or phrase you want to look up in the text box labeled 1. For our example, type in "**saving document**." As soon as you type the words in, the index moves to the topics matching your terms. To display information about a topic found in the index, select the topic by clicking on it, then click on the **Display** button at the bottom of the dialog box.

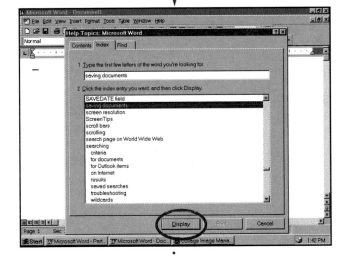

12 Another dialog box appears on your screen detailing the help topic you selected. Read through the information, then click on the **Close** button when you're ready to exit the dialog box. ■

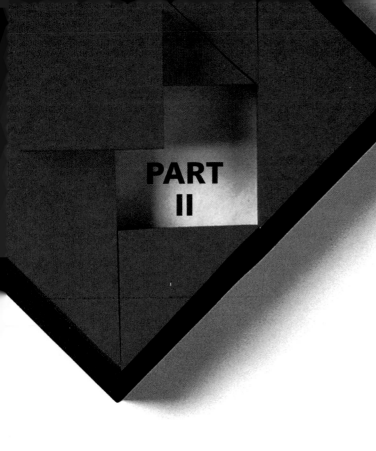

PART II

Entering and Editing Data

Part II: Entering and Editing Data

I N PART I OF THIS BOOK, you learned how to work with the various elements on the Word 97 screen. Now it's time to enter text, learn techniques for building a document, and learn about moving around a document page.

It's easy to enter text with Word; just start typing. An insertion point, which appears as a blinking vertical line in the document area of the window, moves along to the right of the text you type in. You don't have to worry about reaching the end of the line because Word automatically wraps the text to the next line for you. You don't have to press Enter after each line of text. The only time you press Enter is when you want to start a new paragraph.

As you're entering text, there are times when you'll want to insert or delete a line or word you don't want. To do this, you'll need to learn how to move around the document page, select text, and apply editing techniques.

For a simple editing technique, there's nothing better than the Backspace key. When you want to delete a word you just typed, press the Backspace key until the characters are erased. Another good technique to learn is how to use the Insert and Overtype modes.

There are many ways to move around the document. The fastest way is to use your mouse. You can also use the arrow keys on the keyboard to move one character at a time. You can even use key combinations to quickly move around the document. If you prefer to navigate around the document with the keyboard, use the following arrow keys and key combinations:

Navigating Word 97 Using the Keyboard

To move	Press
Right one character	→
Left one character	←
Up one line	↑
Down one line	↓
To the previous word	Ctrl+←
To the next word	Ctrl+→
To the beginning of a line	Home
To the end of a line	End
To the beginning of the document	Ctrl+Home
To the end of the document	Ctrl+End
To the previous screen	PgUp
To the next screen	PgDn

If you want to type over existing text, use Overtype mode. Press the Insert key on your keyboard to turn off Insert mode and toggle to Overtype mode. Then click your mouse pointer where you want to type over existing text and begin typing. When you want to go back to Insert mode again, just press the Insert key to toggle back.

Aside from simple editing techniques, this part of the book will also show you how to move, copy, or delete words and paragraphs using the Cut, Copy, and Paste commands. These commands are used throughout most Windows programs. The tasks that you will learn in this part will save you much time and effort when entering and editing text into your documents. One of the most basic techniques to learn is selecting or highlighting text. Once you've selected text to edit, you can then apply all kinds of Word features, such as moving and copying text, making the text bold, or realigning a single paragraph.

Entering Text

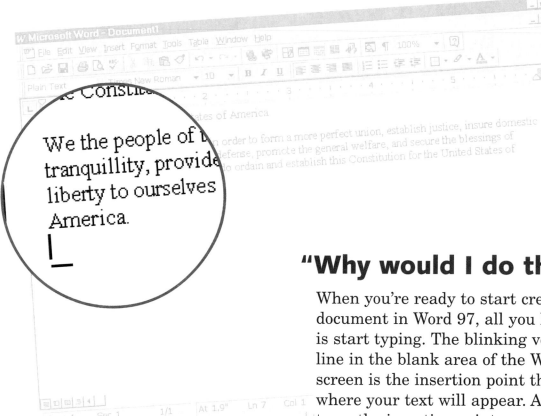

"Why would I do this?"

When you're ready to start creating a document in Word 97, all you have to do is start typing. The blinking vertical line in the blank area of the Word screen is the insertion point that marks where your text will appear. As you type, the insertion point moves to the right. When you reach the right margin, Word automatically wraps the text onto the next line (known as *word wrap*). When you reach the end of a paragraph and want to start a new paragraph, press the **Enter** key.

In the following task, you'll learn how to enter text and create a new paragraph.

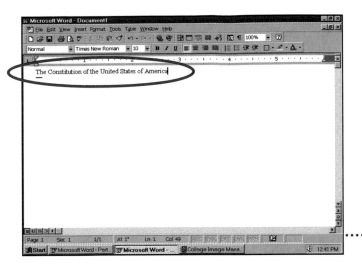

1 If your document has a title, type it in. For example, type in the title that appears in the figure so that your computer screen matches the screen in this book.

Puzzled?

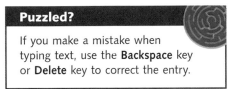

If you make a mistake when typing text, use the **Backspace** key or **Delete** key to correct the entry.

2 When you reach the end of the first line, press **Enter**. Pressing **Enter** ends the paragraph and starts a new paragraph. Notice that the insertion point moves to the beginning of the next line.

Missing Link

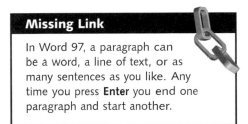

In Word 97, a paragraph can be a word, a line of text, or as many sentences as you like. Any time you press **Enter** you end one paragraph and start another.

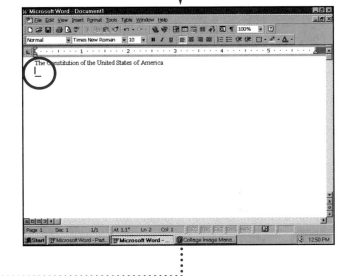

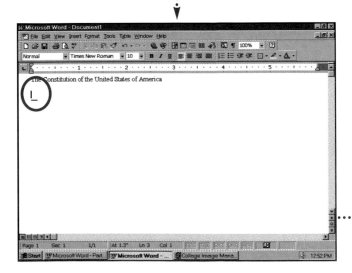

3 Press **Enter** again and Word inserts a blank line below the title. Pressing **Enter** twice creates more space between paragraphs.

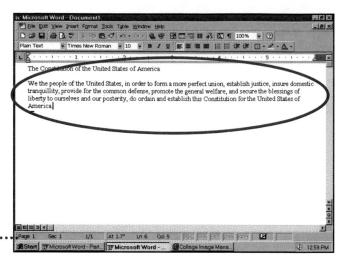

4 Type in the first paragraph that appears in the figure. Remember, you don't have to press **Enter** at the end of a line. Word 97 automatically wraps the text to the next line.

5 When you're ready to type in the next paragraph, press **Enter**. The insertion point moves to the next line. Now you've got the hang of it, right? ■

Puzzled?

Why are some words underlined with a red wavy line? Word's automatic spell checking feature finds and underlines misspelled words as you type. This feature is turned on by default. To turn it off, open the **Tools** menu and select **Options**. Click the **Spelling & Grammar** tab and deselect the **Check spelling as you type** check box.

Moving Around the Document

"Why would I do this?"

The more data you enter into a document, the longer it becomes. Inevitably, you'll need to move around in the document to view different portions of your text. It's also necessary to move around the various areas of the document to make changes to your text. Using a mouse is often the easiest way to move around the document—simply use the vertical or horizontal scroll bar to see other portions of the document.

A scroll bar has arrows for moving around as well as a scroll box you can reposition. You can also click within the scroll bar to move around a document in increments. In this task, you'll practice scrolling using the vertical and horizontal scroll bars.

Task 10: Moving Around the Document

1 The scroll bar arrows provide a speedy way to view a document. To see how it works, click twice on the down scroll arrow at the bottom of the vertical scroll bar (the bar at the right side of the Word 97 window). Clicking the down scroll arrow moves the document down one or more lines at a time.

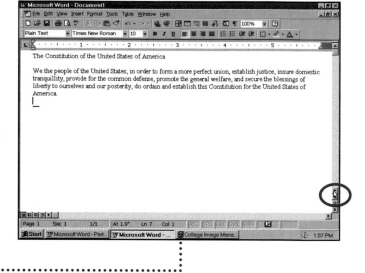

Missing Link

You can point to the up, down, left, or right scroll bar arrow and hold down the left mouse button to scroll the document.

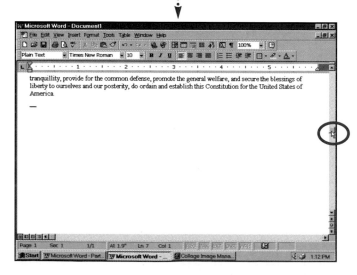

2 Click twice on the up scroll arrow at the top of the vertical scroll bar. Clicking the up scroll arrow scrolls the document up one or more lines at a time, depending on the length of the document.

3 Click halfway down in the vertical scroll bar itself. Clicking within the scroll bar moves the document up or down one window length at a time, rather like stops an elevator makes at various floors.

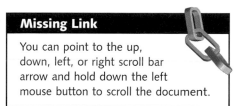

Missing Link

If you're using the new Microsoft IntelliMouse, you can use the wheel to scroll up and down the scroll bars. To scroll up, just roll the wheel forward using your finger (the mouse stays stationary), to scroll down, roll the wheel backward. To scroll in any direction, including horizontally, hold down the wheel button and move the entire mouse.

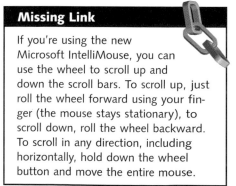

42

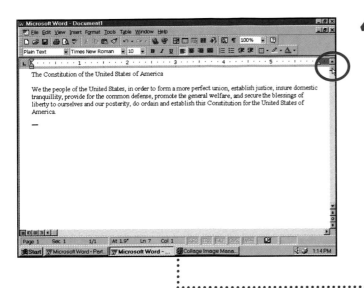

4 Drag the scroll box up to the top of the vertical scroll bar. Dragging the scroll box moves the document quickly to a new location depending on the direction you drag the scroll box. In this case, Word moves the document up to the top of the screen and displays the beginning of the document.

Puzzled?

If you run out of room to move the mouse on your desktop or mouse pad, just lift the mouse and then put it down. The mouse pointer will not move when the mouse is in the air.

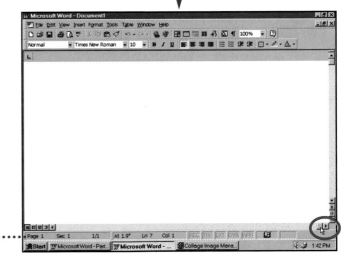

5 Now let's practice with the horizontal scroll bar (located at the bottom of the Word window). Drag the scroll box to the far right of the horizontal scroll bar. Word 97 moves the document to the far left of the screen and displays the right side of the document.

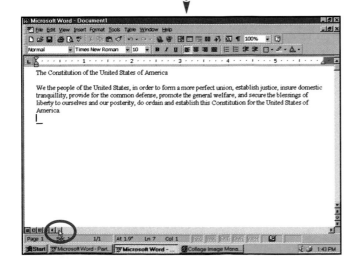

6 Drag the horizontal scroll box to the far left of the bar. Word moves the document to the far left of the screen and displays the left side of the document. ■

Missing Link

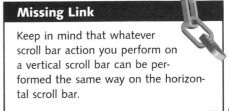

Keep in mind that whatever scroll bar action you perform on a vertical scroll bar can be performed the same way on the horizontal scroll bar.

Inserting and Overwriting Text

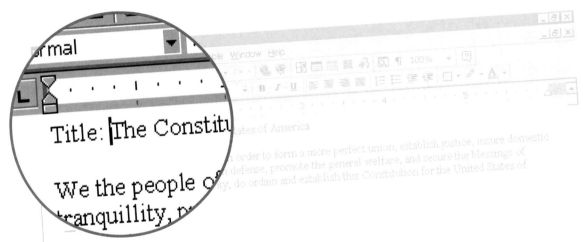

"Why would I do this?"

When entering and editing text you type in, there are two different typing modes you can use: Insert mode and Overwrite mode. By default, Word 97 is in Insert mode when you start the program. In Insert mode, you type text at the insertion point and the existing text moves forward to make room for the new text. Insert mode works like a bulldozer pushing the text aside to make room for new words or characters.

On the other hand, Overwrite mode plows over existing text erasing characters as you go along. Overwriting text

means replacing the existing text with new text.

You can turn the Insert/Overwrite modes on or off with the Insert key on your keyboard. To switch to Overwrite mode, press the **Insert** key. When Overwrite mode is on, the letters **OVR** in the status bar are bolded—this is called an indicator. To switch back to Insert mode, press **Insert** again.

In this task, you'll learn how to insert new text using Insert mode, then learn how to toggle over to Overwrite mode and type over text.

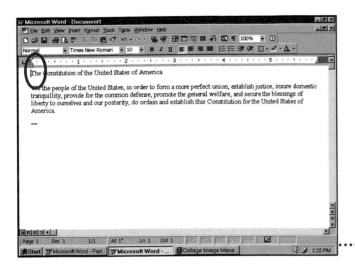

1 Click before the word **The** in the title. This step places the insertion point where you want to insert text.

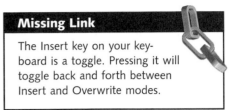

Missing Link

The Insert key on your keyboard is a toggle. Pressing it will toggle back and forth between Insert and Overwrite modes.

2 Type **Title:** Then, press the space bar. This step inserts the new text and pushes the existing text to the right with a space between the new text and the original text.

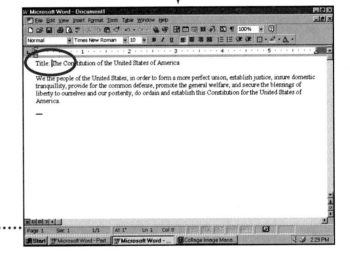

3 Now let's try overwriting text. Click before the **U** in **United**. This step places the insertion point where you want to overwrite text.

4 Press the **Insert** key on your keyboard. This step turns on Overwrite mode. The indicator **OVR** appears in the status bar at the bottom of the screen. This mode overwrites rather than inserts text.

Missing Link

You can also select the text you want to replace and start typing. The new text replaces all the selected text.

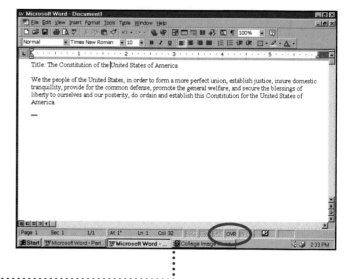

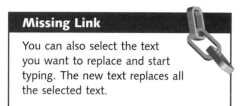

5 Type **USA** and press the space bar. Word 97 deletes the original text and replaces it with **USA**. To erase the rest of the line, press the **Delete** key.

6 Press **Insert** again. The indicator **OVR** disappears in the status bar. Overwrite mode is turned off. ■

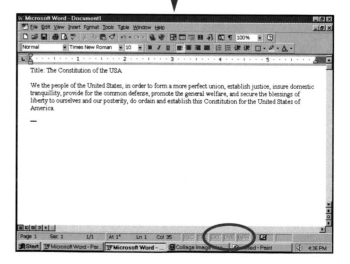

Creating and Combining Paragraphs

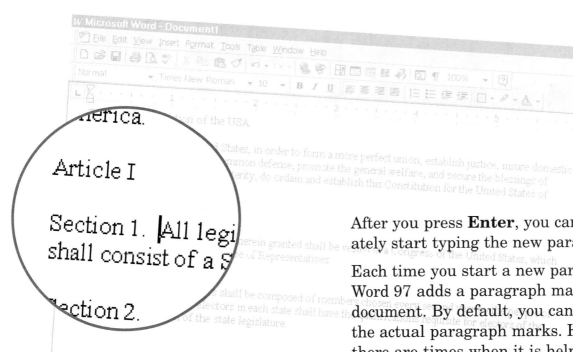

"Why would I do this?"

You learned about creating paragraphs in Task 9, "Entering Text." Now it's time to learn more. To create a new paragraph in your document, press the **Enter** key. This is called a hard return, and it moves the insertion point to the beginning of the next line. Press **Enter** to insert a hard return at the end of a short line, to place a blank line between paragraphs, or to end a paragraph.

After you press **Enter**, you can immediately start typing the new paragraph.

Each time you start a new paragraph, Word 97 adds a paragraph mark to the document. By default, you cannot see the actual paragraph marks. However there are times when it is helpful to view the paragraph marks.

There are also times when you may want to combine two separate paragraphs into one or separate an existing paragraph into two paragraphs. In either case, all it takes is a quick placement of the insertion point and a press of the **Enter** or **Backspace** key. Let's practice separating a paragraph, combining paragraphs, and viewing paragraph marks.

1 Click after the last line in the second paragraph, then press **Enter** twice. Pressing **Enter** ends the current paragraph and starts the next paragraph, even if the next paragraph is a blank line.

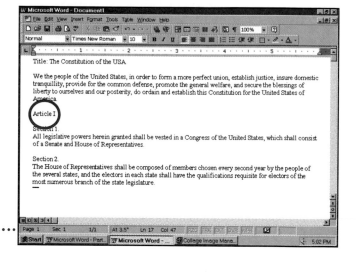

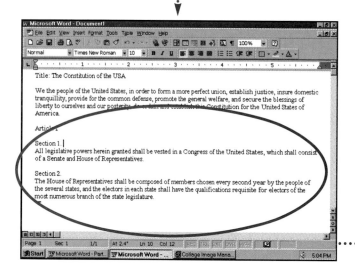

2 Type in the next five paragraphs shown in the figure so your screen matches the one in this book.

3 Word inserts a paragraph mark in the document each time you press **Enter**. By default, paragraph marks do not appear on-screen. If you want to display paragraph marks, click the **Show/Hide** button on the Standard toolbar.

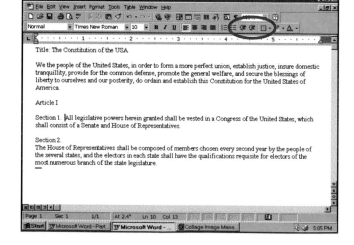

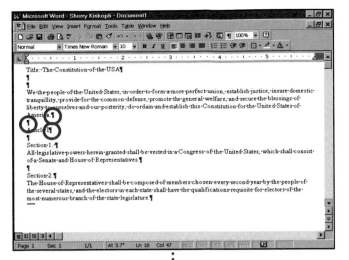

4 Now you can see the paragraph marks in your document. If you want to turn them off again, click on the **Show/Hide** button.

Missing Link

Some people like to see the paragraph marks as they work in their document. The marks make it easy to see where paragraphs begin and end. If you prefer not to see the paragraph marks, click the **Show/Hide** icon to turn them off.

5 Now let's practice combining paragraphs. Click after **Section I**. This places the insertion point at the end of the paragraph, which in this case is simply two words. Be sure to click after the period.

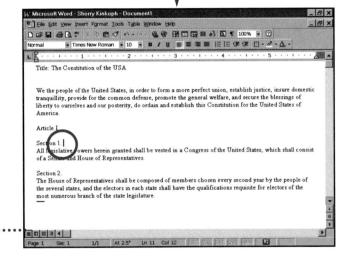

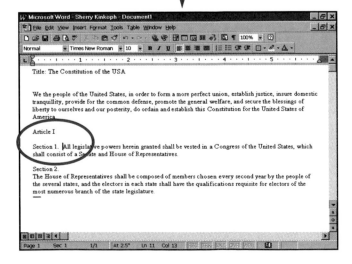

6 Press **Delete**. Pressing the **Delete** key deletes the paragraph mark at the end of the current paragraph and the paragraph from below moves up to join the current paragraph. Press the **Spacebar** to separate the two paragraphs as sentences. ■

Missing Link

To split the paragraphs, place the insertion point where you want the break to appear. Then, press **Enter**. Press **Enter** twice to place an extra line between the paragraphs.

49

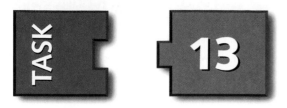

Selecting Text

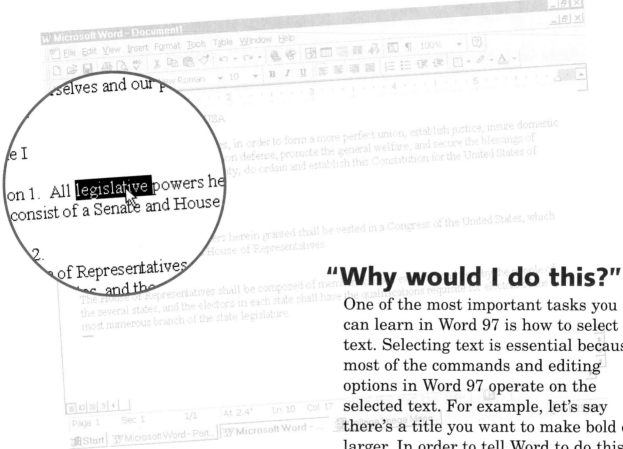

"Why would I do this?"

One of the most important tasks you can learn in Word 97 is how to select text. Selecting text is essential because most of the commands and editing options in Word 97 operate on the selected text. For example, let's say there's a title you want to make bold or larger. In order to tell Word to do this, you must first select the text you want to change. You can select any amount of text: a block of text, a word, a line, a sentence, or a paragraph. The easiest way to select text is with the mouse.

First let's select a section of text with the mouse. Next, we will select a word, then a line of text, a sentence, a paragraph, and a block of text.

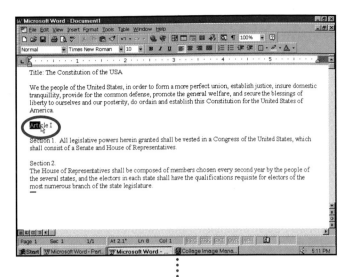

1 Place the mouse pointer at the beginning of the text you want to select, hold down the left mouse button, and drag the mouse pointer across the text you want to select. Notice the text you drag over is automatically selected.

Puzzled?

If you selected the wrong text, simply click on any text in the document. Then start over.

2 Double-click anywhere in the word **legislative** in the fourth paragraph. This step selects only a word of text.

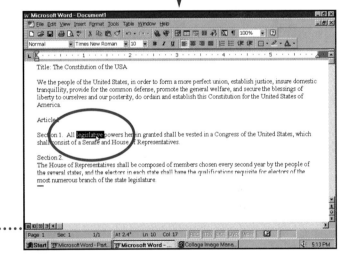

3 You can select an entire line of text by clicking in the far left margin next to the line you want to select. For example, click the left margin next to the words **Section 1** in the fourth paragraph. This step selects a line of text.

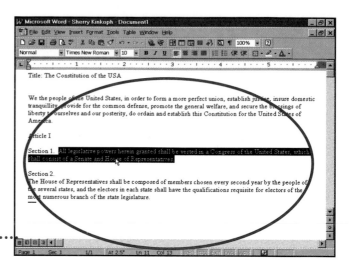

4 Hold down **Ctrl** and click anywhere within the sentence. This step selects a sentence.

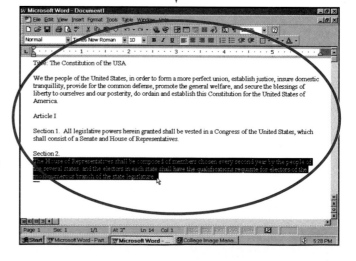

5 Double-click the left margin next to the paragraph. This step selects a paragraph.

Missing Link

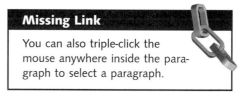

You can also triple-click the mouse anywhere inside the paragraph to select a paragraph.

6 You can also select a block of text without dragging. Position the mouse pointer at the beginning of the text you want to select, click the left mouse button, and then hold down the **Shift** key as you click the end of the block of text. This highlights the text from the first click to the second click. ■

Deleting Text and Using Undo

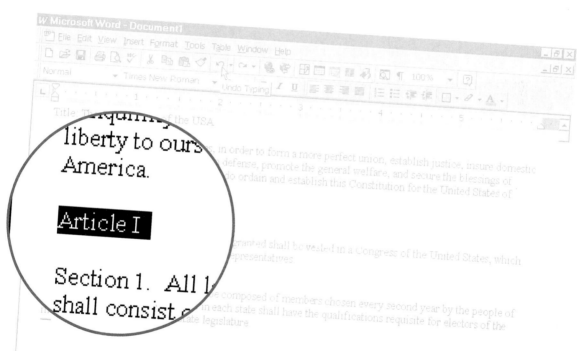

"Why would I do this?"

Sometimes text you initially typed into the document is incorrect and needs to be changed. You've already learned one way to get rid of text you no longer want—turn on the Overwrite mode and overwrite the existing text with new text. You can also select the text you want to remove and press the Delete key on your keyboard. To delete one character, use the Backspace key.

While any of those methods will work, there's yet another way you can fix your text. You can use the Undo command. The Undo feature recovers the most recent changes to document text, such as restoring deleted text that you did not intend to delete. You'll find the Undo command on the Standard toolbar and in the Edit menu. In this task, you'll learn how this feature works.

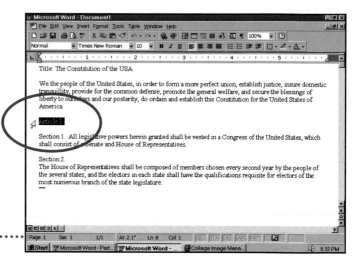

1 Click the left margin next to the text **Article I**. This step selects the text you want to delete.

2 Press **Delete**. Word for Windows deletes the text. The remaining text moves up (or over) to fill in the gap.

3 Click the **Undo** icon (the button that contains an arrow that curves to the left and down) on the Standard toolbar. Clicking the **Undo** button selects the Undo command. Word for Windows restores the deleted text. As you can see, the document returns to its original form. Click outside the selected text to deselect the text. ■

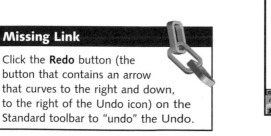

Missing Link

Click the **Redo** button (the button that contains an arrow that curves to the right and down, to the right of the Undo icon) on the Standard toolbar to "undo" the Undo.

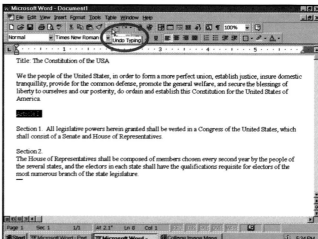

Copying Text

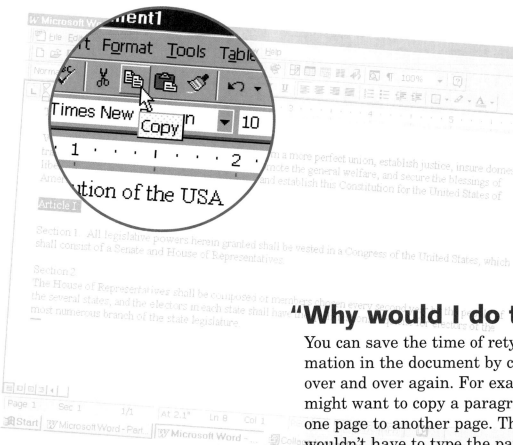

"Why would I do this?"

You can save the time of retyping information in the document by copying text over and over again. For example, you might want to copy a paragraph from one page to another page. That way, you wouldn't have to type the paragraph over again, saving you time and keystrokes.

You can use Word's Copy and Paste commands to copy text. You'll find these commands available on the Standard toolbar as well as in the Edit menu. In this task, you'll practice copying text from one area of your document into another.

1 Select the text you want to copy. For our example, click the left margin next to **Article I**. This highlights the paragraph we're going to copy.

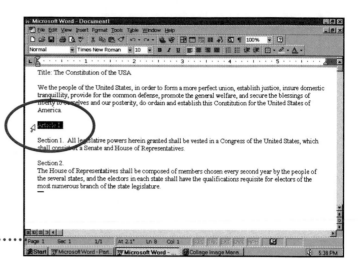

2 Click the **Copy** icon (the button that contains two pieces of paper) on the Standard toolbar. Clicking the Copy button copies the text to the Clipboard. The Clipboard is a temporary holding area for text and graphics.

3 Click at the end of the document, below the last paragraph. This step places the insertion point where you want the copied text to appear.

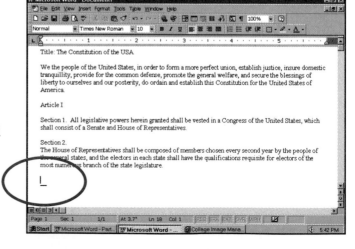

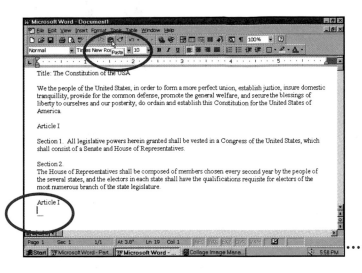

4 Click the **Paste** icon (the button that contains a piece of paper on top of a clipboard) on the Standard toolbar. Clicking the Paste button selects the Paste command. The copied text now appears in the new location (as well as the original location).

5 Click after the **I** in **Article I** in the newly copied text.

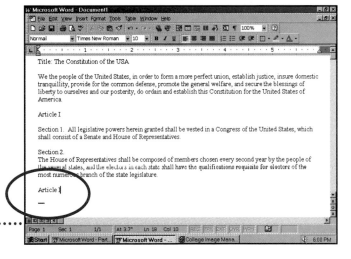

6 Type another **I** to make the text read **II**. This step changes the article number. ■

Puzzled?

If you copied the wrong text or copied the data to the wrong location, click the **Undo** button on the Standard toolbar to undo the most recent copy. Then, start over. Or, just delete the copied text.

TASK 16

Moving Text

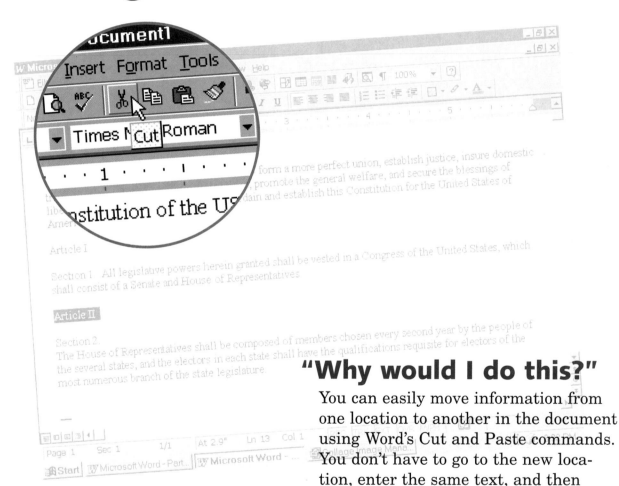

"Why would I do this?"

You can easily move information from one location to another in the document using Word's Cut and Paste commands. You don't have to go to the new location, enter the same text, and then erase the text in the old location. For example, you might want to swap the order of paragraphs, or you might want to move text in a document because the layout of the document has changed. In this task you'll learn how to move text around in your document.

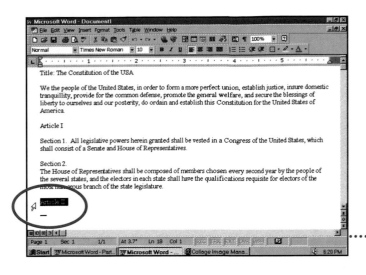

1 Select the text you want to move. In our example, click the left margin next to **Article II**. This selects the text.

2 Click the **Cut** icon (the button that contains a scissors) on the Standard toolbar. Clicking the **Cut** button cuts the text from the document and places it on the Clipboard (a temporary holding area).

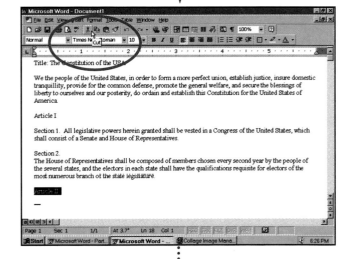

Missing Link

You can also use the **Ctrl+X** and **Ctrl+V** key combinations to select the Cut and Paste commands.

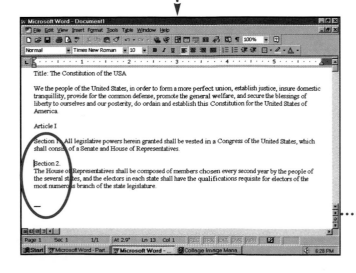

3 Click at the beginning of the fifth paragraph, the one that starts with **Section 2**. This step places the insertion point where you want to move the text.

4 Click the **Paste** icon (the button that contains a piece of paper on top of a clipboard) on the Standard toolbar to paste the text in the new location.

Missing Link

To use drag-and-drop to move the text, select the text. Click and hold down the mouse button. You see a small box under the mouse pointer. Drag the text to the new location. Release the mouse button.

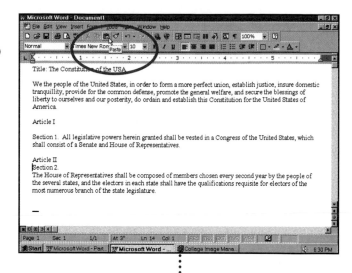

5 The text now appears in the new location. If necessary, press **Enter** to insert a hard return to separate the newly moved text and the existing paragraph.

6 To undo the move completely, click on the **Undo** button three times. This will return your document screen to where it started in step 1. ■

Puzzled?

If you moved the wrong text or moved the text to the wrong location, click the **Undo** button on the Standard toolbar to undo the most recent move. Then, start over.

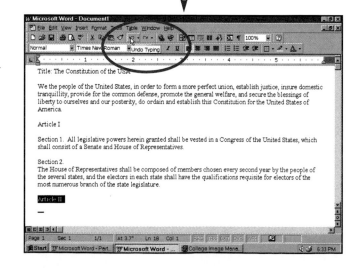

Inserting a Tab

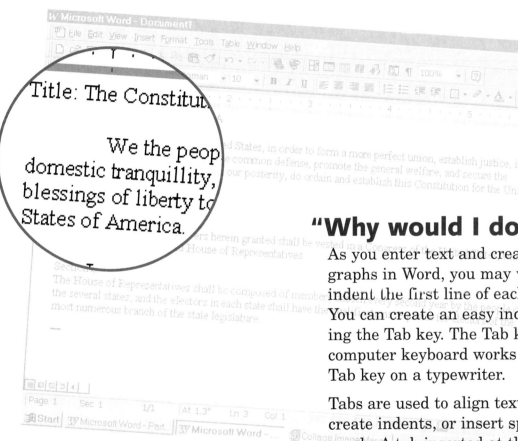

"Why would I do this?"

As you enter text and create paragraphs in Word, you may want to indent the first line of each paragraph. You can create an easy indent by pressing the Tab key. The Tab key on your computer keyboard works just like the Tab key on a typewriter.

Tabs are used to align text in columns, create indents, or insert space between words. A tab inserted at the beginning of a paragraph will indent the text from the left margin. Tabs used in a memo heading can insert space between the headings and the memo information. You'll learn how to set tabs in Part IV, "Setting Tabs," but let's learn how to insert a simple tab now so you can indent any paragraphs you type.

Task 17: Inserting a Tab

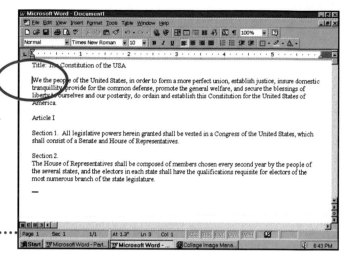

1 Click before **We** in the first sentence of the second paragraph. This places the insertion point where you want to insert a tab (at the beginning of the paragraph).

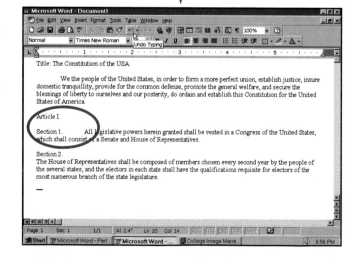

2 Press **Tab** on the keyboard. Pressing Tab inserts a tab and moves the insertion point to the next tab stop. As you can see, the first sentence begins at the tab stop. Word provides a default tab stop every 1/2 inch. You can also change the tab settings, which you'll learn to do in Task 32 in Part IV.

3 Now let's try inserting a tab within a paragraph. Click before the word **All** in the fourth paragraph (right after Section 1.) and press the **Tab** key. The text shifts over the space of the tab. To undo a tab, press the **Backspace** key or click on the **Undo** icon in the Standard toolbar. ■

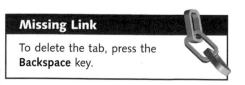

Missing Link

To delete the tab, press the **Backspace** key.

Inserting a Page Break

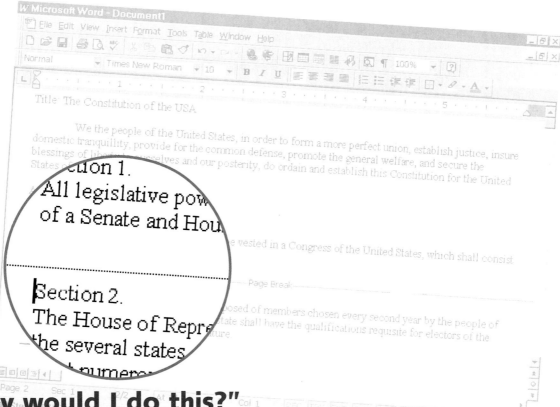

"Why would I do this?"

When the text reaches the end of a page, Word inserts a soft page break and starts a new page. A soft page break appears as a dotted line across the Word 97 screen separating the text. You can continue typing page after page of text and Word will automatically break the text into pages for you. If you go back later and insert additional text into the first page, the existing text shifts and the document repaginates, adjusting the locations of the soft page breaks.

There are occasions when you'll want your page to end at a certain place, without relying on Word's soft page breaks. In such cases, you'll need to insert a hard (manual) page break. Manual page breaks override automatic (soft) page breaks entered by Word.

Task 18: Inserting a Page Break

1 Click before the fourth paragraph, the one starting with the words **Section 2**. This step places the insertion point where you want the new page to begin. Remember that you can place the insertion point by using the mouse or the arrow keys.

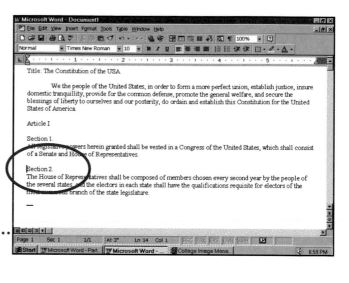

2 Press **Ctrl+Enter**. Pressing **Ctrl+Enter** inserts a hard page break in the document. A dotted line appears with the words Page Break in the middle, as you can see in the figure. When you print the document, a new page will begin where you inserted the page break.

3 To remove the page break, click the **Undo** button on the Standard toolbar immediately after inserting the page break. Or, click on the page break to select it and press **Delete**. ■

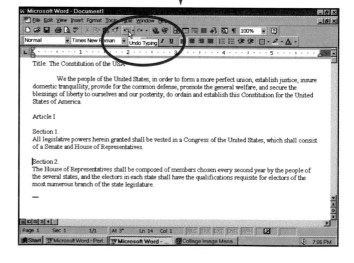

Going to a Specific Page

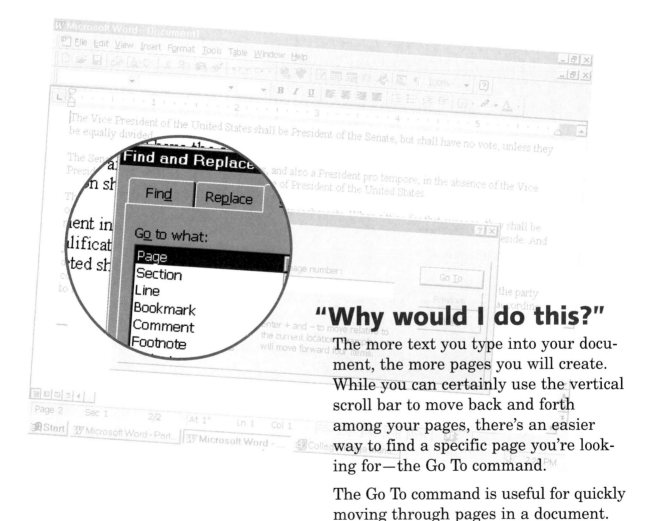

"Why would I do this?"

The more text you type into your document, the more pages you will create. While you can certainly use the vertical scroll bar to move back and forth among your pages, there's an easier way to find a specific page you're looking for—the Go To command.

The Go To command is useful for quickly moving through pages in a document. You can jump to any page that is out-of-view in the current document. Perhaps you're working on page 4 and you want to make a change on page 1. You can use the Go To command to get there.

1 Open the **Edit** menu and select **Go To**. This selects the Go To command.

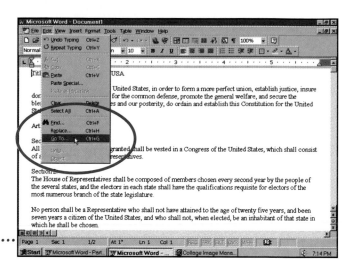

2 Word 97 opens the Find and Replace dialog box, with the Go To tab at the front of the dialog box. (If the Go To tab isn't at the front, just click on the **Go To** tab name.)

Missing Link

Notice that the Go To tab has other elements you can go to besides document pages. You can also use this tab to locate footnotes, sections, and more.

3 Click inside the **Enter page number** text box and type in the page number you want to turn to, then click on the **Go To** command button. Word 97 displays the page you specified. Click the **Close** button to close the dialog box. ■

Puzzled?

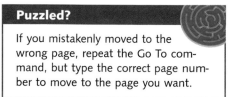

If you mistakenly moved to the wrong page, repeat the Go To command, but type the correct page number to move to the page you want.

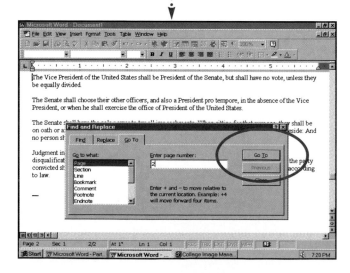

PART III

Managing Word 97 Files

AFTER YOU START CREATING DOCUMENTS with Word 97, you'll want to save them so you can open them again. This part of the book gives you the nitty-gritty details about managing document files in Word 97. You'll learn how to save your work, cancel a document, close a document, open a document, find a document, and create a new document.

In the first task, you'll learn how to use Word's Save command to store your document on your computer's hard disk drive. Unless you save your work, you won't see it again. When you save your document, you're actually creating a file stored on a computer disk. There are many different types of files you can save on your computer. Files created in a word processing program, like Word 97, are usually labeled with the file extension *.doc*. Files extensions are simply three letters added at the end of a file name, preceded with a dot, that designate what type of file it is. On the following page, you will find a handy chart of different file types you might use when working with Word 97.

By default, Word automatically saves your work to a backup file every 10 minutes. The backup file's name consists of the same name as your original document except that the backup file type is *.BAK* (for example, *LETTER.BAK*). If your power goes off and you turn on your computer, Word opens the backup file automatically.

The very first time you save a file, you must assign it a name. When you're working with a previously saved file, you don't have to rename it each time you save it. All you have to do is instruct Word to save the file, and it saves the version you currently have displayed on the screen. If you want to save an existing file under a new name, yet retain the original, you can do so with the Save As command. Saving a file with a new name gives you two copies of the same document with differences in their data.

File Types

File extension	Description
.doc	Document file, commonly created in word processing programs
.txt	Plain text file, common on the Internet and among e-mail programs
.pcx	Graphics file containing pictures or illustrations
.gif	Another type of graphics file
.htm	Plain ASCII text files, usually found on the Internet
.zip	A file that's been compressed to save space

After saving and closing your Word files, you'll want to open them again to work on them some more. To open a file, use the Open command. This command opens a dialog box where you can see a list of files you've previously saved.

Word 97 also has two features that can help you with creating a document: templates and wizards. A *template* provides a pattern for shaping a document. The template contains boilerplate text, styles, glossary items, macros, a menu, key, and Toolbar assignments. A *wizard* is a special template that guides you through the creation of a document, step by step. It displays dialog boxes, messages, and graphics that tell you how to fill in a template or create forms.

After completing the tasks in this part, you'll have the necessary skills to manage files in Word 97.

Saving a Document

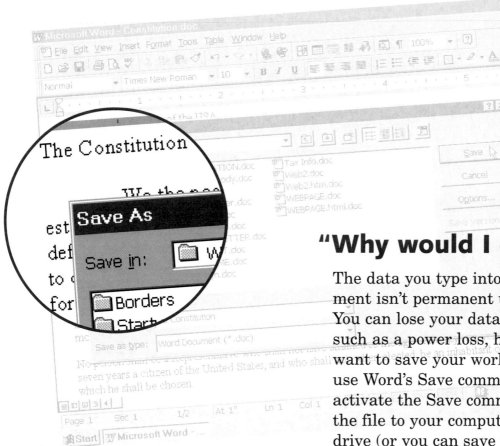

"Why would I do this?"

The data you type into a Word 97 document isn't permanent until you save it. You can lose your data if something, such as a power loss, happens. If you want to save your work, you'll need to use Word's Save command. When you activate the Save command, Word saves the file to your computer's hard disk drive (or you can save the data to a floppy disk). When you need the document again, you can retrieve it easily.

It's a good idea to save your work every few minutes, as well as at the end of a work session. Once you've saved your work, you can then close the document to clear the screen, or exit the program. In this task, you'll learn the basics of saving Word 97 documents.

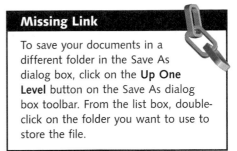

1 To save a new file, click the **Save** icon on the Standard toolbar. Word displays the Save As dialog box. From this box, you can assign file names, file types, and designate in which folder and drive you want the file stored.

> **Missing Link**
>
> To save your documents in a different folder in the Save As dialog box, click on the **Up One Level** button on the Save As dialog box toolbar. From the list box, double-click on the folder you want to use to store the file.

2 In the **File Name** text box, type in a name for your document. For example, in Part II we worked on typing in the United States Constitution. You might want to save that file as **CONSTITUTION**. You can type as many characters as you want for the file name.

> **Puzzled?**
>
> If you type a file name that already exists, Word displays an alert box that asks **Replace existing file?** Click **Cancel** to return to the Save As dialog box and then type a new name.

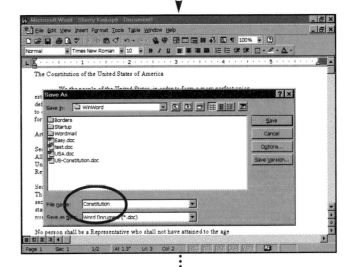

3 Click on the **Save** command button. This step accepts the file name and returns you to the document. The new file name now appears in the title bar of the Word window.

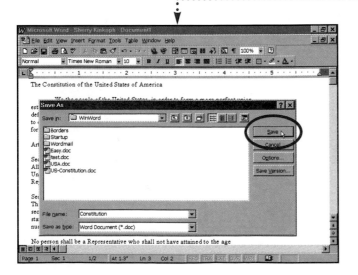

> **Missing Link**
>
> You can even assign a password to your document. In the Save As dialog box, click on the **Options** button. This opens the Save box with options for controlling how files are saved. At the bottom of the box are options for assigning a password to the file. To reopen the file again, you'll need to type in the correct password.

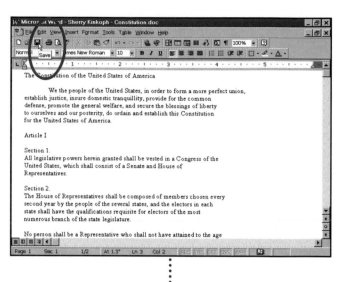

4 If you're working on a saved file, you don't have to assign the file a name again. Click the **Save** icon in the Standard toolbar and Word saves the file without opening the Save As dialog box.

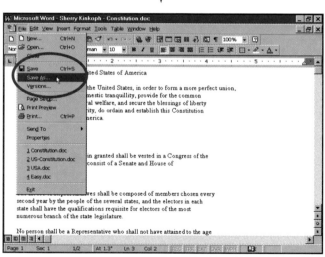

5 To save a new version of the document, but with a different name, open the **File** menu and select the **Save As** command. This opens the Save As dialog box.

6 In the Save As dialog box, type a new name in the **File Name** text box (delete or type over the existing file name). If necessary, you can also choose a different file type, drive, and folder from the appropriate drop-down lists. Click **Save** when you're ready to exit the dialog box. ■

Missing Link

When naming files, use only alphanumeric characters in the file name. Don't use spaces or punctuation marks. You can type either upper- or lowercase characters. Don't worry about adding file extensions. Word 97 automatically adds the .DOC extension to your documents.

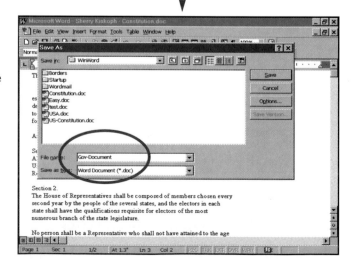

Closing a Document

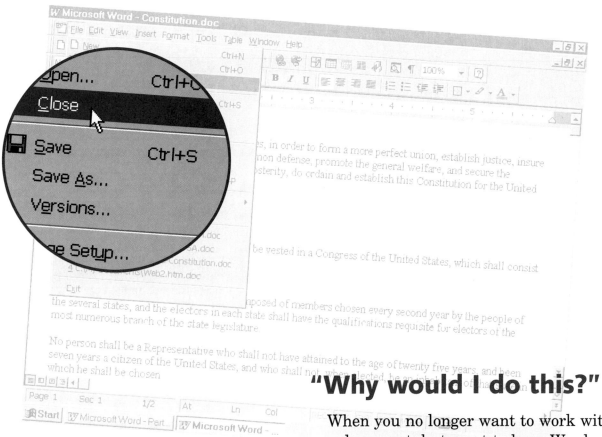

When you no longer want to work with a document, but want to keep Word open, you can close the document using the Close command. You then can use the Open button on the Standard toolbar to open another document, or use the New button on the Standard toolbar to create a new document. You can open more than one document at once; you don't have to close a document before opening another.

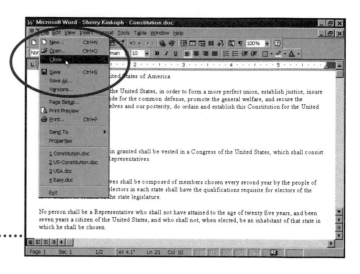

1 To close a document, open the **File** menu and select **Close**.

2 Word closes the current document. If you were only working with one document, the screen empties and you now see a blank gray area. You can choose to open another document or create a new document.

Missing Link

You can also click on the document window's **Close** button (**X**) to close a file. It's located at the far right end of the menu bar.

3 If you have made changes to the file before closing it, and haven't saved the changes, Word displays an alert box. Choose **Yes** to save the changes and close the document. If you don't want to save the changes, choose **No** to ignore them and close the document. ■

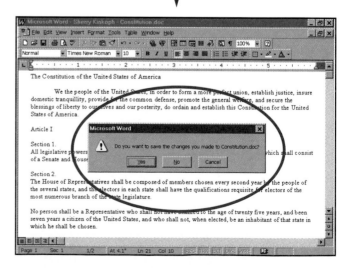

Missing Link

When Word displays the alert box and you're not sure about saving the changes or not, just click the **Cancel** button and Word keeps the file open. You can then look over the document and see if you want to keep the changes.

Opening a Document

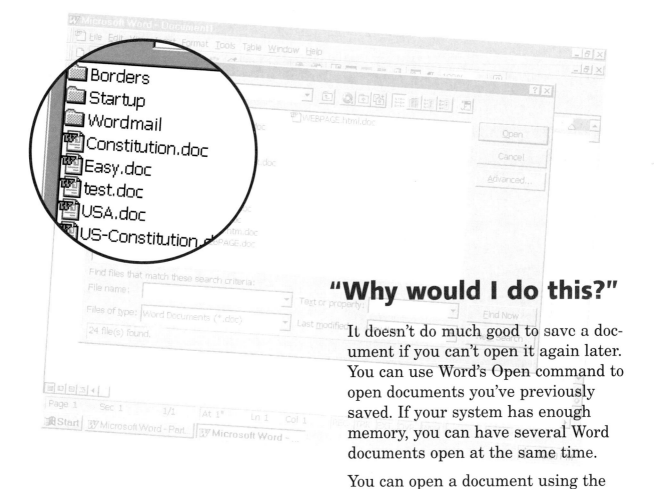

"Why would I do this?"

It doesn't do much good to save a document if you can't open it again later. You can use Word's Open command to open documents you've previously saved. If your system has enough memory, you can have several Word documents open at the same time.

You can open a document using the Open command on the File menu, or you can click on the Open icon on the Standard toolbar. Either method displays the Open dialog. From there you can locate the exact file you want to view in the Word window.

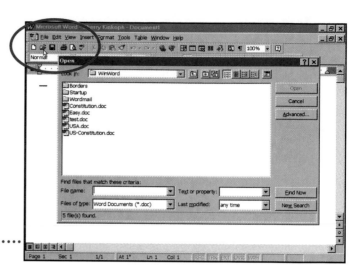

1 Click the **Open** icon on the Standard tool-bar. Word opens the Open dialog box.

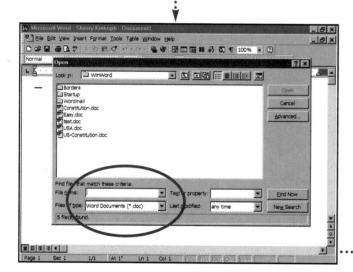

2 If you know the name of the file you want to open, type its name into the **File Name** text box.

3 You can also select the file name from the List box. Just click on the file you want to open.

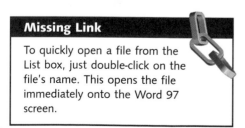

Missing Link

To quickly open a file from the List box, just double-click on the file's name. This opens the file immediately onto the Word 97 screen.

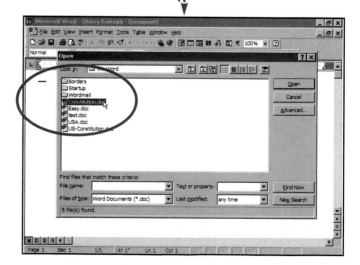

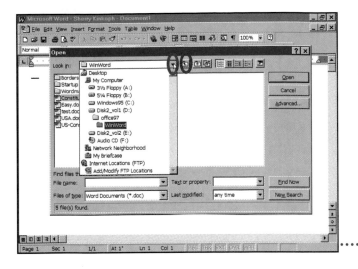

4 If you don't see the file listed in the List box, click the drop-down arrow at the end of the **Look In** box and switch to another folder. To move up a folder level, click the **Up One Level** button on the Open dialog box toolbar. Once you locate the file, click on it.

5 To preview a file before opening it, click the **Preview** button on the Open toolbar. Word displays the document in the Preview window on the right side of the Open dialog box.

> **Missing Link**
>
> You can use the scroll bar in the Preview window to scroll through the document. To close the Preview window, click on the **List** button in the Open dialog box toolbar (the fourth button from the left).

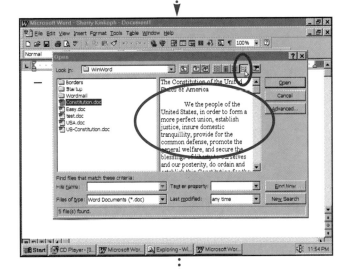

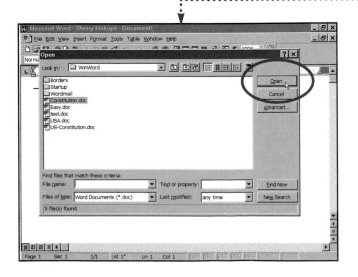

6 When you're ready to open the file, click the **Open** command button. Word displays the document on-screen. The file name appears in the title bar. ■

> **Missing Link**
>
> The most recently used files appear at the bottom of the File menu. To open a file quickly, click **File** and then click the file you want to open.

Creating a New Document

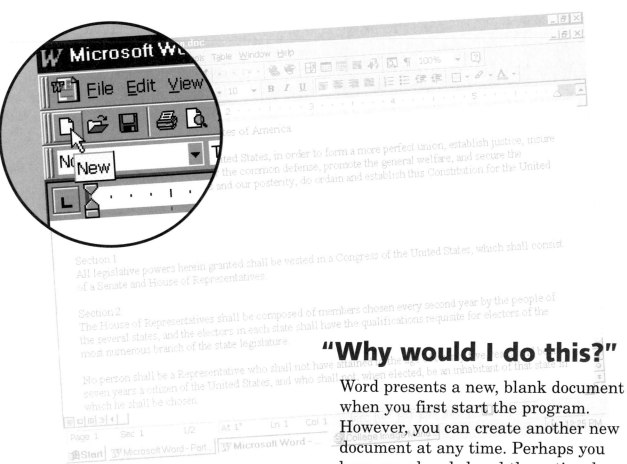

"Why would I do this?"

Word presents a new, blank document when you first start the program. However, you can create another new document at any time. Perhaps you have saved and closed the active document and want to begin a new one.

It's easy to create a new document, even if you have several existing documents still open. You can create a new document by clicking on the New icon in the Standard toolbar.

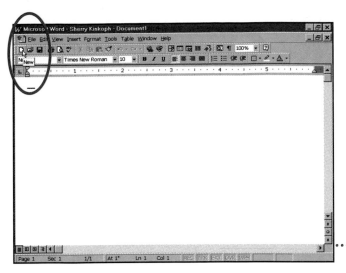

1 Click the **New** icon on the Standard tool-bar.

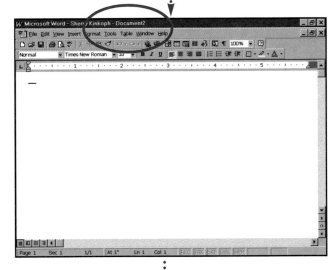

2 A blank document appears on-screen. This document is titled DOCUMENT2 (the number varies depending on the number of documents you have created during this session). Notice the name appears in the title bar.

3 To close the document, click on the document's **Close** button, located on the far right side of the menu bar. Word closes the document. ■

Missing Link

If you have more than one document open, you can switch among documents by choosing **Window** on the menu bar. Then choose a document from the list at the bottom of the Window menu. Use this method to switch between open documents.

TASK 24

Finding a Document

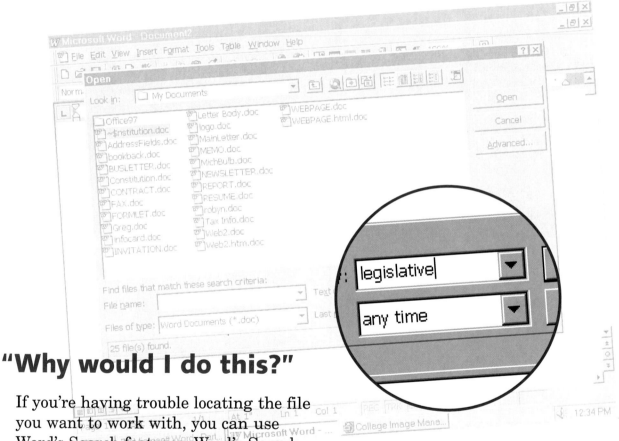

"Why would I do this?"

If you're having trouble locating the file you want to work with, you can use Word's Search features. Word's Search for Files feature enables you to search for a single file or group of files based on search criteria you specify. When Word finds the files, you can preview and open the document. The Search for Files feature is handy when you can't remember the name of a file.

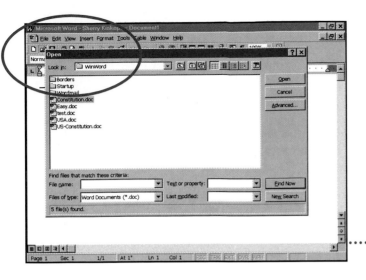

1 Click the **Open** icon on the Standard toolbar. This displays the Open dialog box.

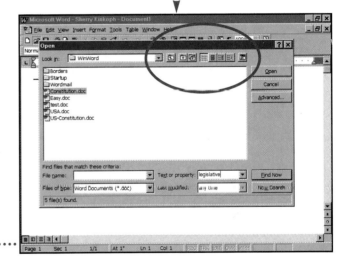

2 Select the drive or folder you want to search. For example, click the **Up One Level** button on the Open dialog box toolbar and specify the drive or folders you want to search.

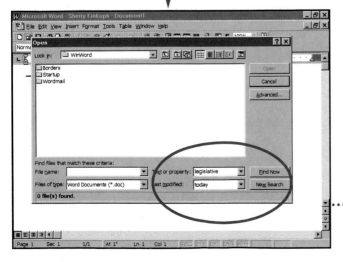

3 Type the word you're looking for in the **Text or Property** text box at the bottom of the Open dialog box. This step enters the search criteria.

> **Missing Link**
>
> To search for subfolders, click the **Commands and Settings** button on the Open dialog box toolbar. Then choose **Search Subfolders** from the menu.

4 Click the **Find Now** button in the Open dialog box. Word displays a list of files that match your search criteria.

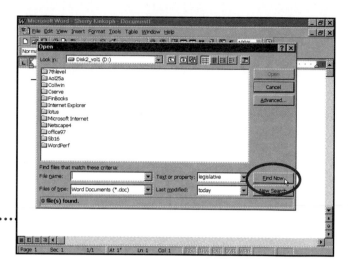

5 You can use the Last Modified drop-down box to specify a time frame for your search. For example, click the **Last modified** drop-down arrow and choose **Today** if you want to locate specific files you've worked on today.

6 To open a file, select it and click on the **Open** button. To start a new search if the first one wasn't successful, click the **New Search** button. This step clears the search criteria in the Text or Property and Last Modified text boxes. To close the Open dialog box without making any changes, click the **Cancel** button. ■

Puzzled?

When Word doesn't find any files based on the specified search criteria, just click the **New Search** button and try again.

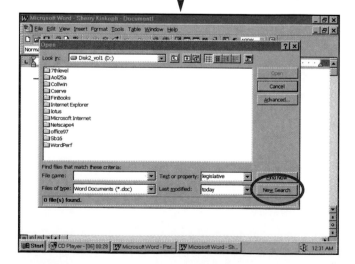

Using a Template

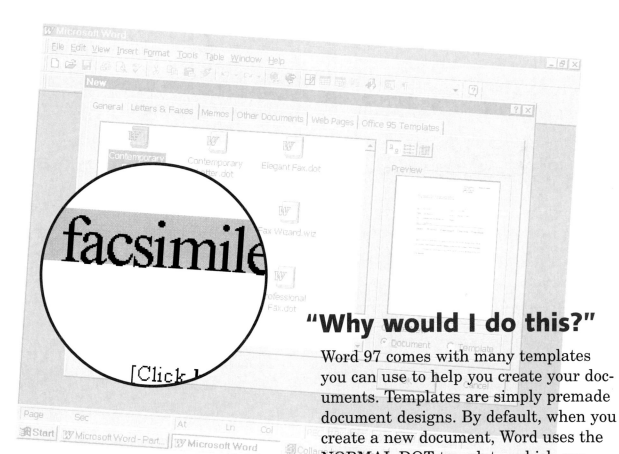

"Why would I do this?"

Word 97 comes with many templates you can use to help you create your documents. Templates are simply premade document designs. By default, when you create a new document, Word uses the NORMAL.DOT template, which contains the standard document settings. Word also provides several families of templates that are organized in categories: General, Other Documents, Letters & Faxes, Memos, Reports, and Office 95 Templates. You can use a template at any time to standardize types of documents that you frequently use.

Task 25: Using a Template

1 Pull down the **File** menu and select **New**. The New dialog box appears on your screen.

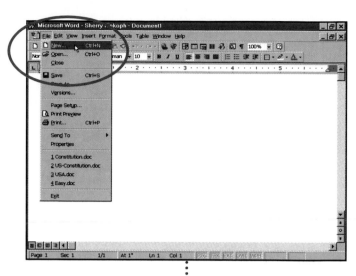

Puzzled?

When you create a new document based on a template, you must use the File, New command, not the New button on the Standard toolbar. The New button doesn't display the New dialog box.

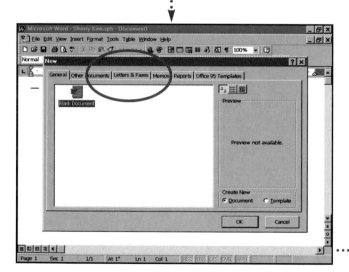

2 Choose a template category you want to use by clicking on a tab name. For example, click the **Letters & Faxes** tab. You see icons that represent various letters and faxes.

3 The **Letters & Faxes** tab appears at the front of the dialog box. Notice there are several different templates to choose from. Use the scroll bar to move up and down the listing.

Missing Link

Templates labeled with the *.dot* extension will open directly onto your Word 97 screen. If you choose a template with a *.wiz* extension, this opens a Template Wizard, a step-by-step feature that walks you through the creation of a template. You'll learn about Template Wizards in the next task.

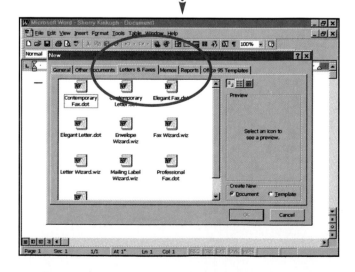

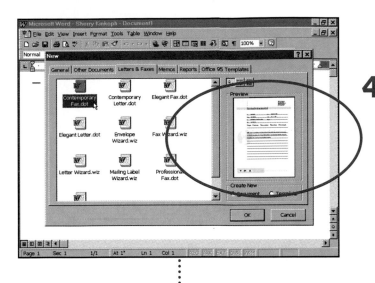

4 Select the template icon you want to use. For example, the **Contemporary Fax** template is selected in the figure. When you click on a template, a sample appears in the Preview window on the right side of the New dialog box.

5 When you're ready to open the template, click **OK**. Word 97 displays a new document with placeholder text that helps you get started. This is a copy of the template, not the original template.

> **Puzzled?**
>
> If you don't want to use the template you selected, click on the document's **Close** button.

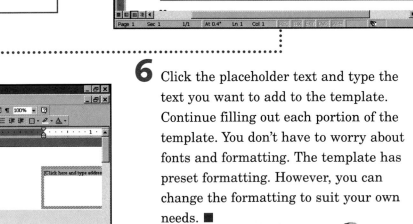

6 Click the placeholder text and type the text you want to add to the template. Continue filling out each portion of the template. You don't have to worry about fonts and formatting. The template has preset formatting. However, you can change the formatting to suit your own needs. ■

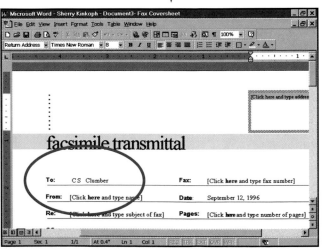

> **Missing Link**
>
> To save a document that is based on a template, open the **File** menu and select the **Save** command. You save the document containing the template just as as you would any other document.

87

Using a Wizard

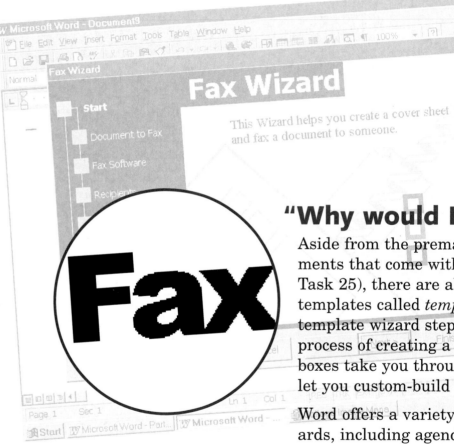

"Why would I do this?"

Aside from the premade template documents that come with Word 97 (see Task 25), there are also several special templates called *template wizards*. A template wizard steps you through the process of creating a document. Dialog boxes take you through each step and let you custom-build your document.

Word offers a variety of template wizards, including agendas, awards, calendars, resumes, fax cover sheets, legal pleading papers, letters, memos, newsletters, and tables. Wizard templates are easily identified by the .wiz extensions added to the template's name. Just choose the wizard you want and get a running start on creating a professional-looking document.

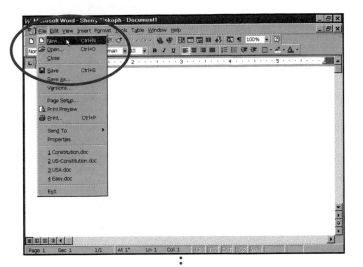

1 Open the **File** menu and select **New**. This opens the New dialog box.

Puzzled?

You can only access the New dialog box by opening the **File** menu and clicking on **New**. Clicking on the **New** icon on the Standard toolbar only opens a new, blank document onto your screen.

2 You'll find wizard templates scattered among the many template tabs. Wizard templates have a *.wiz* extension added to their names. For our example, click the **Letters & Faxes** tab. Select the **Fax Wizard.wiz** template and click the **OK** button.

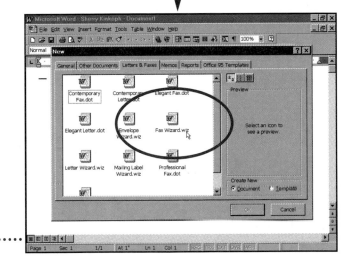

3 Word 97 displays the first wizard dialog box. To continue, click on the Next button.

4 Another dialog box appears with options or directions for you to follow. Make your selections and click on the **Next** button to continue.

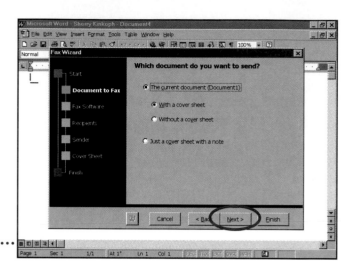

5 Follow the steps in each wizard dialog that appears to create your new document. Press **Next** to move through the rest of the screens. In the last dialog box, click on the **Finish** button.

6 The template appears on your Word 97 screen. You can now fill in each place-holder, if necessary, or make any changes to existing text. To save the file, click on the **Save** toolbar icon and give the file a new name. ■

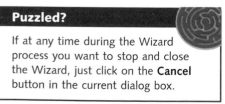

Puzzled?

If at any time during the Wizard process you want to stop and close the Wizard, just click on the **Cancel** button in the current dialog box.

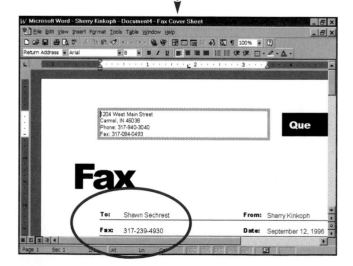

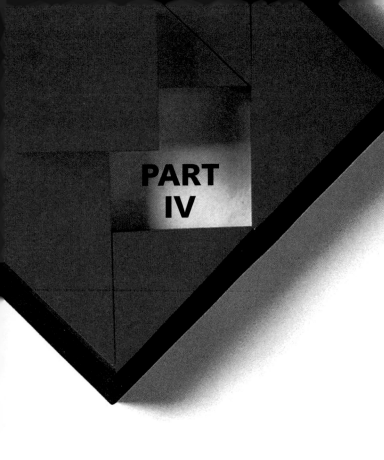

PART IV

Formatting Your Document

WITHOUT FORMATTING, your documents would all look the same. *Formatting* refers to the changes you can make to the appearance of text in your documents. Thankfully, Word 97 offers you a variety of formatting tools you can use to make your documents more attractive and readable. And what kind of formatting tools will you find in Word?

If we were to take a poll and find out which formatting is applied the most, the results would probably be the boldface, italics, and underlining.

For that very reason, the creators of Word have placed buttons for these options up front and center, easily accessible with a click of your mouse button. The formatting tools you'll use the most are conveniently located on the Formatting toolbar. The Formatting toolbar, found directly below the Standard toolbar, has controls for setting fonts, font sizes, alignment and more.

For example, if you want to make your report's heading stand out from the rest of the text, select the text and click on the **Bold** button. Another click on the button turns the option off again. You can do the same with the **Italic** button.

By default, the **Underline** button enables you to underline text in your document with a simple underline (also called an *underscore*). But if you prefer a different underline style, you can open the Font dialog box and choose from a list of styles.

When it comes to dressing up a document, fonts are the way to go. A font is a style of type in a particular typeface and size. Fonts can be fancy or plain and can visually set the mood for your document.

Word displays various fonts and font sizes in two drop-down lists at the far left side of the Formatting toolbar. You can also open the Font dialog to make changes to your fonts and sizes, as well as preview your selections before actually assigning them.

Another part of formatting your documents is being able to reposition your text on a page. By default, Word is set up to align your text to the left as soon as you start typing in a document. Left alignment means that text is aligned flush with the left margin, with a "ragged right" edge. Center alignment centers text between the left and right margins. Right-aligned text appears flush with the right margin. Justified text spreads text between the left and right margins by expanding or contracting the space between words.

Aside from the alignment buttons, you can also control alignment with tabs, indents, line spacing, and margins.

- Margins are the edges of your document page. If you ever have trouble fitting your text on a page, try changing the top, bottom, left, and right margins.

- Indents effect the placement of paragraphs. You can indent paragraphs from the left, right, or both margins. You can also indent only the first line of the paragraph.

- One of the most basic ways to indent a paragraph is to press the **Tab** key.

- Tabs are also useful for lining up columns of text. The easy way to set tab stops is to use Word's ruler. You just select the tab style you want and click it in place on the ruler. You can also specify tab stops and styles in the Tabs dialog box.

- Adding bullets or numbers to a list can really make the list stand out. You can choose the type of bullet that you want to insert for a bulleted list or choose the type of numbering scheme you want to use in a numbered list.

There are a lot of different ways you can control the appearance of your Word documents. With a little practice you'll soon be using the formatting tools to make your documents look great.

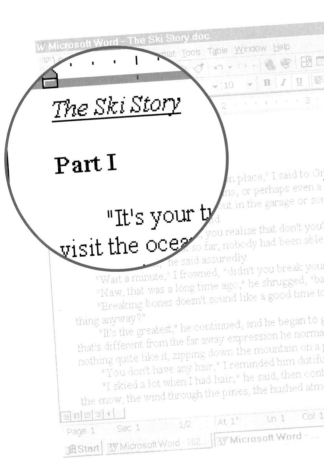

Making Text Bold, Italic, and Underlined

"Why would I do this?"

To bring attention to important text in a document, you can make text bold, italic and underlined. These are three of the most basic formatting commands people use when creating a document. For example, you might want to make the title of a book italic, or you might need to make the word "don't" bold in a letter to your kids. Or perhaps you want to underline a statistic in the office report you're typing.

You can easily activate any of these formatting commands by clicking on the appropriate toolbar button. You can choose to apply these commands before typing in the text you want to format (simply turn the formatting feature on before entering text), or you can select existing text and then apply the appropriate commands.

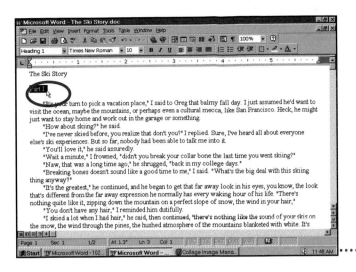

1 First, select the text you want to format.

Missing Link

You can also turn on a formatting tool before you actually type in text. For example, if you know you want the next word to appear in boldface type, click on the **Bold** toolbar button before typing the word. This turns the feature on. After typing the word, click the **Bold** button again to toggle it off.

2 To make the selected text bold, click the **Bold** button (the button with the 'B' on it) on the Formatting toolbar. This action applies bold to the selected text.

Missing Link

You can also press **Ctrl+B** to select the Bold command using the keyboard.

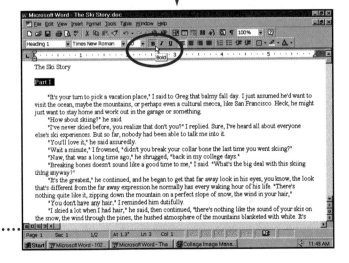

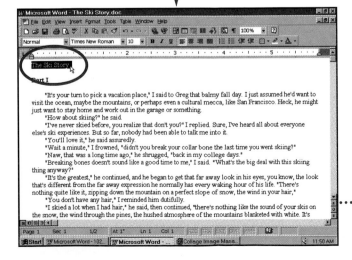

3 Now let's try using the Italics command. Select a word or phrase you want to italicize.

4 Click the **Italic** button (the button with an italicized 'I' on it) on the Formatting toolbar. This activates the Italics feature and italicizes the text.

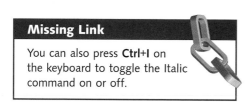

Missing Link

You can also press **Ctrl+I** on the keyboard to toggle the Italic command on or off.

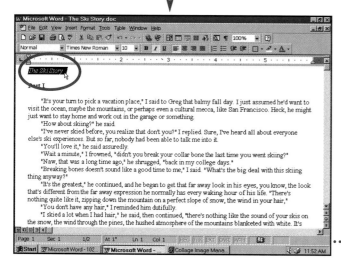

5 Select a word or sentence you want to underline.

6 Click the **Underline** button on the Formatting toolbar. This underlines the selected text. Click outside the selected text to deselect the text. ■

Missing Link

You can also press **Ctrl+U** to select the Underline command.

Puzzled?

To undo the bold, italic, or underline styles, click the **Undo** button on the toolbar immediately after applying the format.

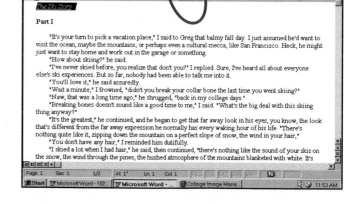

Changing the Font and Font Size

"Why would I do this?"

To draw attention to important words and phrases in a document or to set apart different sections of your page, you can change the font and font size. Word offers you a variety of fonts to choose from, and many different font sizes to use.

By default, Word starts you out with the *Times New Roman* font style and 10-point type size. However, that's awfully small, and not so easy to read. You can change the fonts and sizes used throughout your document to suit your needs. For example, if you're writing an article, you might want to set the title in italics and underline it. You might also want to increase the font size so the title is larger than the rest of the article.

1 To change the font of existing text, first select the text you want to change.

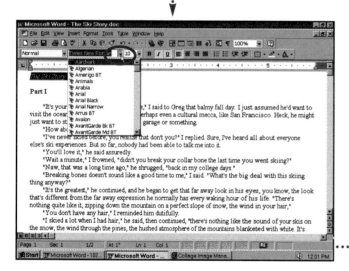

2 Click the down arrow button next to the Font box on the Formatting toolbar. This displays the list of fonts.

Puzzled?

The fonts in the list can vary, depending on your printer and the fonts you've installed under Windows 95.

3 Click any font in the list. This changes the font for the selected text.

Missing Link

It's never a good idea to use too many different fonts in a single document. If you vary the styles too much, it may make the document hard to read. Experiment to see what fonts work best, and study other printed materials, such as books or magazines, to see what appeals to readers.

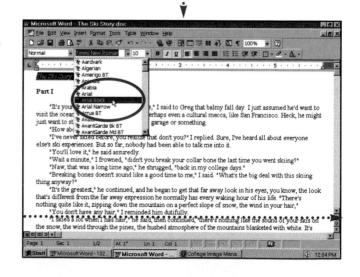

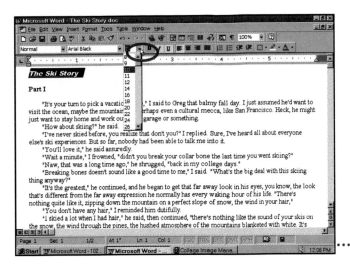

4 To change the font size of the selected text, click the down arrow button next to the Font Size box on the Formatting toolbar. This displays the list of font sizes.

5 Click on the new font size you want to use. In the example shown, I chose 16 point type. The higher the font size number, the larger the type will appear on the document page.

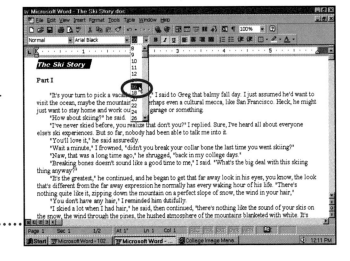

6 Click outside the selected text to deselect the text. The newly formatted text will reflect your changes. Notice in the example shown, the text appears wider, taller, and bigger than it was before. ■

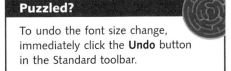

Puzzled?

To undo the font size change, immediately click the **Undo** button in the Standard toolbar.

Changing Text Alignment

"Why would I do this?"

By default, when you enter text into a document, text automatically aligns flush with the left margin. You can change the alignment of text at any time. For example, you might want to center an article's title, or you may want to set a return address flush right with the right margin.

You can use Word's alignment commands to reposition text horizontally across a page. You'll find four alignment buttons on the Formatting toolbar: Left, Center, Right, and Justified. Left alignment lines up the text at the left margin. A right alignment lines the text flush right with the right margin. Center alignment centers the text in the middle of the page. Justified alignment will flush the text with both the left and right margins with the words spread out evenly in between.

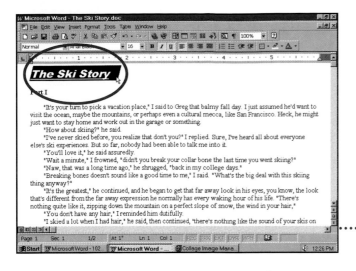

1 Select the text you want to align.

2 To right-align the text, click on the **Align Right** button on the Formatting toolbar. This activates the right alignment command and flushes the text right with the right margin.

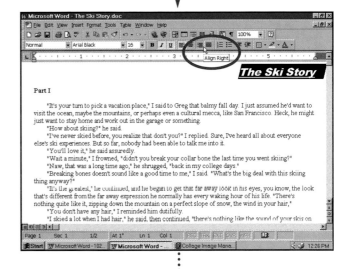

Missing Link

You can also use keyboard shortcuts to align text. Press **Ctrl+R** to right-align a paragraph of text. Press **Ctrl+E** to center text.

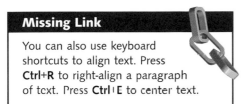

3 To practice centering text on a page, first select the text you want to align; then click on the **Center** button on the Formatting toolbar. This centers the selected text, as shown in the example. Click outside the selected text to deselect the text. ■

Puzzled?

To undo the most recent alignment change, click the **Undo** button on the Standard toolbar.

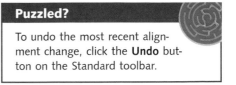

TASK

30

Adding Indents

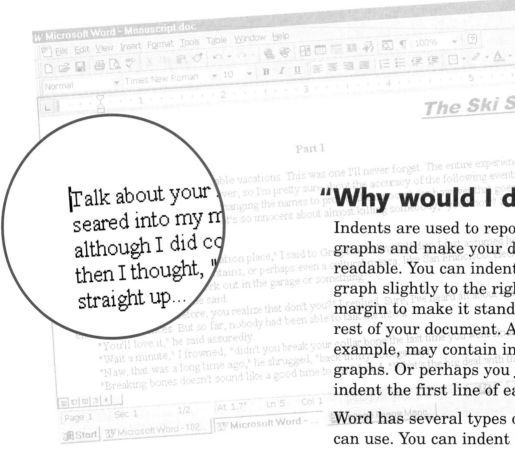

"Why would I do this?"

Indents are used to reposition paragraphs and make your documents more readable. You can indent an entire paragraph slightly to the right of the left margin to make it stand out from the rest of your document. A contract, for example, may contain indented paragraphs. Or perhaps you just want to indent the first line of each paragraph.

Word has several types of indents you can use. You can indent paragraphs from the left or right margins or both at the same time. A hanging indent is another type of indent. It "hangs" the first line of a paragraph to the left and shifts the remaining lines over from the left margin. Hanging indents are useful for bulleted or numbered lists and bibliographic entries. A first line indent only indents the first line of the paragraph.

1 To set a simple indent, click the insertion point in front of the line you want to indent or select the paragraph you want to indent. The indent command you set will apply to the current paragraph you're working with.

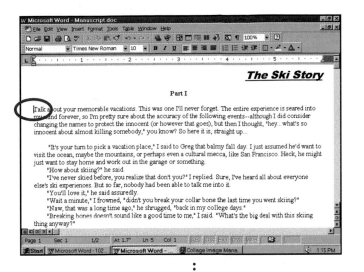

Missing Link

You can choose to indent more than one paragraph at a time. Select the paragraphs you want to indent by using the selecting techniques you learned about in Task 13 in Part II of this book.

2 Click the **Increase Indent** button on the Formatting toolbar. This indents the whole paragraph, by 1/2 inch increments. As you can see, the paragraph is now indented.

Puzzled?

To undo the indent, click the **Undo** button on the Standard toolbar or the **Decrease Indent** button (to the left of the **Increase Indent** button) on the Formatting toolbar immediately.

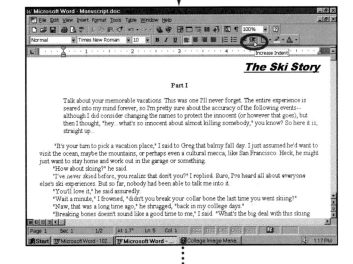

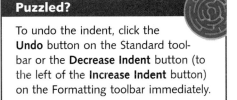

3 If you prefer to set another type of indent, you can open the Paragraph dialog box and make your selection. Click the insertion point in the paragraph you want to indent, and then open the **Format** menu and select **Paragraph**.

Missing Link

To create a simple indent while entering text, just press the Tab key on your keyboard.

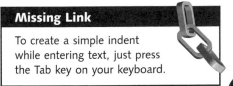

4 In the Paragraph dialog box, click on the **Indents and Spacing** tab to bring its options to the front of the dialog box. This tab has options for setting text alignment and spacing.

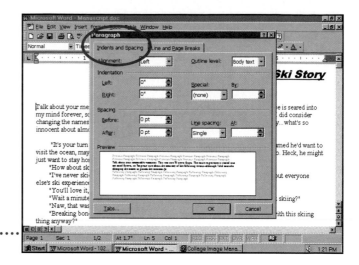

5 To set a specific type of indent, click on the **Special** drop-down arrow in the Indentation area of the dialog box. Click **Hanging**. This selects a hanging indent. The amount to indent by (1/2") is filled in automatically (shown in the **By** text box).

Missing Link

You can also set a specific measurement for your indents using the **Indents and Spacing** tab in the Paragraph dialog box. Use the Indentation controls to set a precise measurement for left or right indents.

6 Click **OK** to exit the dialog box and set the indent into your text. As shown in the example, the first line of the paragraph is flush left, but the remaining lines in the paragraph are "hanging," indented a 1/2 inch. ■

Puzzled?

To undo the indent or hanging indent, click the **Undo** button on the Standard toolbar immediately.

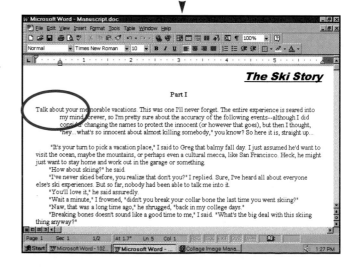

Creating Bulleted and Numbered Lists

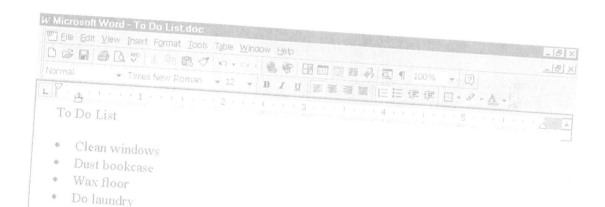

"Why would I do this?"

Bulleted lists and numbered lists are a good way to organize and present a series of data in your document. For example, if you want to make a list of company objectives stand out in a report, you can add bullets to the text. If you're listing steps, you can add numbers to the steps to make them more readable.

You'll find buttons for setting simple bulleted and numbered lists on the Formatting toolbar. Word 97 has additional options for setting specific types of bullets or determining a number series.

Task 31: Creating Bulleted and Numbered Lists

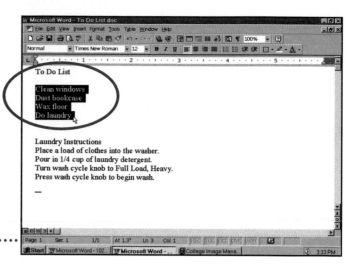

1 To create a bulleted list, first select the paragraphs you want to turn into bulleted text.

2 Click on the **Bullets** button on the Formatting toolbar. This immediately adds bullets to the selected text, as shown in the figure.

Puzzled?

To remove the bullets in the list, immediately click the **Undo** button on the Standard toolbar.

3 If you want to use a specific type of bullet or change the style of the existing bullets, you'll need to open the Bullets and Numbering dialog box. Select the text you want to add bullets to, then open the **Format** menu and select **Bullets and Numbering**.

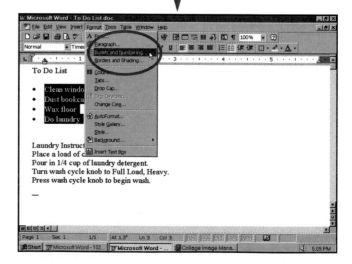

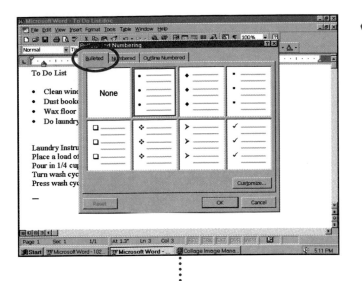

4 In the Bullets and Numbering dialog box, click on the **Bulleted** tab name to bring the bullet options to the front of the dialog box. Click on the bullet style you want to use; then click **OK** to exit the dialog box.

Puzzled?

If you start typing in text after setting a bulleted or numbered list, you may notice Word adds bullets or numbers to the new text. To turn off the bulleted or numbered list feature, click on the **Bullets** or **Numbering** button on the Formatting toolbar.

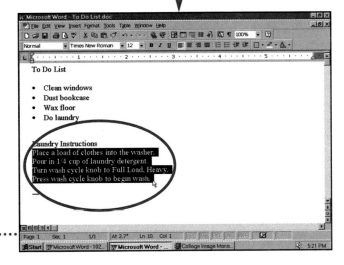

5 To set text as a numbered list, select the paragraphs you want to number.

6 Click on the **Numbering** button on the Formatting toolbar. This adds the appropriate sequence of numbers to the list, as shown in the figure.

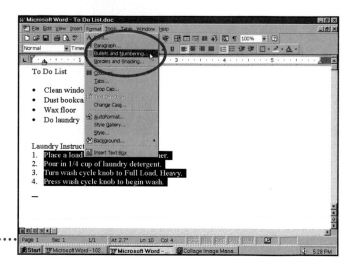

7 If you prefer to use a different numbering style, you must open the Bullets and Numbering dialog box. Right-click on the selected text to open a shortcut menu, then select **Bullets and Numbering**.

8 In the Bullets and Numbering dialog box, click on the **Numbered** tab name to bring the numbering options to the front of the dialog box. Select the numbering style you want to use.

9 Click on **OK** to exit the dialog box. The numbers now appear with your text. If you want to add more text to your list, you don't have to set the numbering options again. Word automatically adds numbers to any text added to the list. To turn the feature off, just click on the **Numbering** button on the toolbar. ■

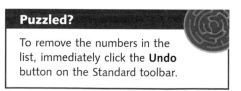

Puzzled?

To remove the numbers in the list, immediately click the **Undo** button on the Standard toolbar.

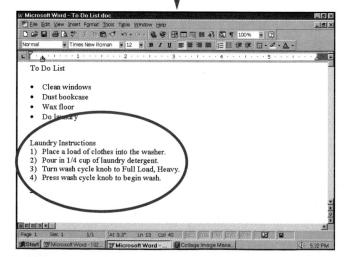

Setting Tabs

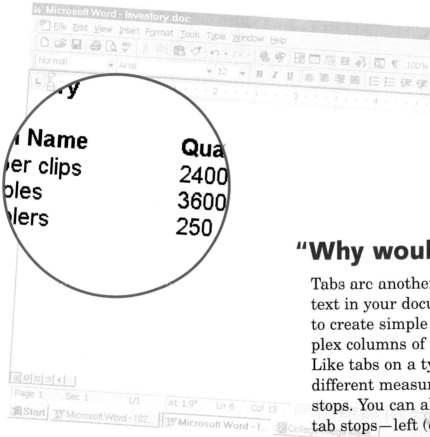

"Why would I do this?"

Tabs arc another method of aligning text in your document. Tabs can be used to create simple indents or to align complex columns of text across your page. Like tabs on a typewriter, you can set different measurements for your tab stops. You can also set different types of tab stops—left (default), right, decimal, or center tabs. You can also insert a dot leader (a continuous line of dots) before a tab stop.

Word 97 lets you set tabs using the horizontal ruler, or you can open the Tabs dialog box and set precise measurements or styles for your tab stops. In this task, you'll learn how to do both.

Task 32: Setting Tabs

1 To set a tab on the ruler, move the insertion point to the beginning of the text where you want to insert a tab stop.

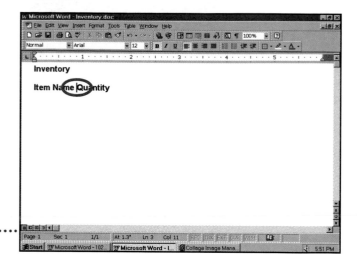

Missing Link

If the ruler is not showing at the top of your screen, open the **View** menu and click on **Ruler**.

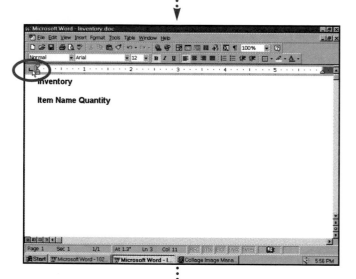

2 At the left edge of the ruler is the Tab Alignment button. The button has a symbol that looks like the letter L on it, which stands for Left tab. To select another type of tab alignment, click on the **Tab Alignment** button to rotate through the four different kinds of tabs and stop when the desired tab symbol appears.

3 After selecting a tab type, click on the ruler where you want the tab stop set. This inserts a tab marker.

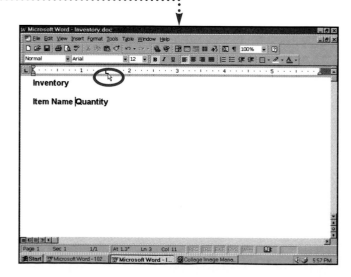

Missing Link

Word 97 provides a default tab stop every 1/2 inch. However, you can set your own tab stop measurements to suit your document's needs.

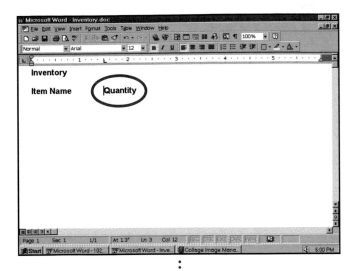

4 To use the new tab stop, press your **Tab** key. Pressing **Tab** moves the insertion point and any text to the right of it to the next tab stop—in this example, the new stop set at 1 1/2 inches.

Puzzled?

If you want to remove the tab stop, select the text for which you set the tab, point to the tab marker and drag it off the ruler. If you want to change the tab's position, drag the tab marker to a new location on the ruler.

5 To set tab stops using the Tabs dialog box, open the **Format** menu and select **Tabs**.

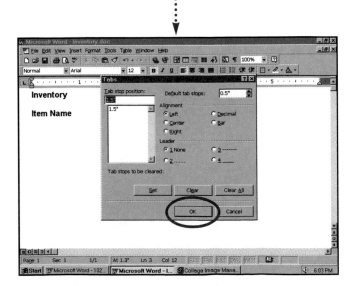

6 From the Tabs dialog box, you can set different types of tab alignments and measurements or set tabs using leader characters (tabs with dots or dashes). You can also specify a different default tab stop measurement. To clear existing tabs you've set on the ruler click on the **Clear All** button. Click **OK** to exit the dialog box. ■

Missing Link

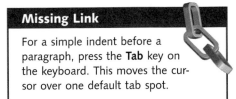

For a simple indent before a paragraph, press the **Tab** key on the keyboard. This moves the cursor over one default tab spot.

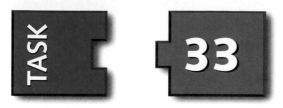

Changing Margins

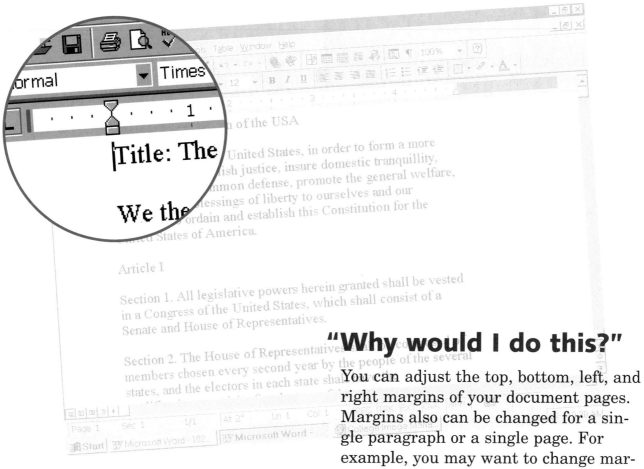

"Why would I do this?"

You can adjust the top, bottom, left, and right margins of your document pages. Margins also can be changed for a single paragraph or a single page. For example, you may want to change margins if you're printing a document onto a sheet of paper that has an existing letterhead or logo. Or maybe your text needs to fit a precise size of paper.

Word lets you change margins using the ruler or you can specify exact margins using the Page Setup dialog box.

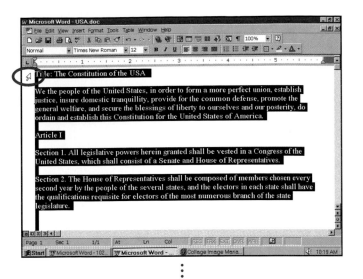

1 To set a margin using the ruler, place the insertion point in the paragraph in which you want the margin changed, or select multiple paragraphs. If you're changing the margin for an entire page, triple-click in the left margin to select the entire document.

Puzzled?

If the ruler isn't showing on your screen, open the **View** menu and select **Ruler**.

2 At the left end of the ruler you'll find the Left margin control. To set a new left margin, click on the **Left Indent** and drag the margin marker to a new setting on the ruler.

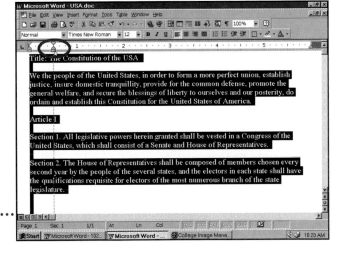

3 When you release the margin marker, the new margin is set.

4 To change top, bottom, or right margins, you must open the Page Setup dialog box. Pull down the **File** menu and select **Page Setup**.

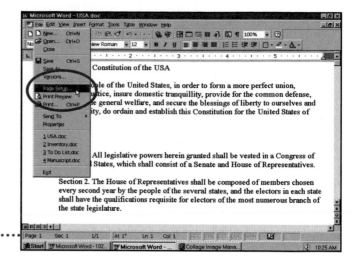

5 You see the Page Setup dialog box. Click on the **Margins** tab to bring its options to the front of the dialog box. The Margins tab has controls for setting all the margins on a page.

6 To set new margins, click on the appropriate up or down arrow next to the margin you want to change. Clicking the up arrow increases the margin measurement; clicking the down arrow decreases it. To apply the margin changes, click on the **OK** button. The new margins are applied to your document. ■

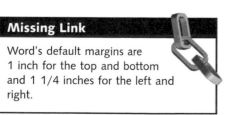

Missing Link

Word's default margins are 1 inch for the top and bottom and 1 1/4 inches for the left and right.

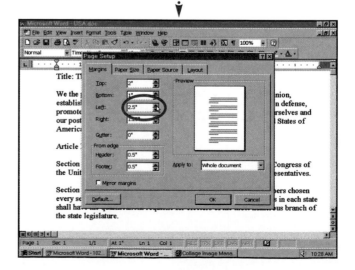

Changing Line Spacing

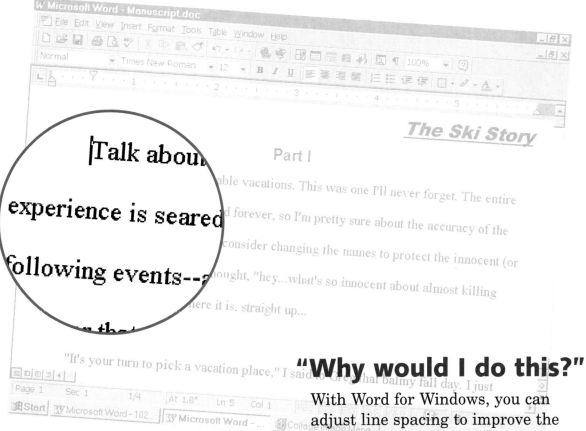

"Why would I do this?"

With Word for Windows, you can adjust line spacing to improve the appearance of a document. The most common line-spacing options include single spacing (default), 1-1/2 lines, and double-spacing. For example, you might want to double-space a draft, a manuscript, or a script so that you can mark your changes more easily on the printed pages.

1 To change the line spacing of your text, first select the text.

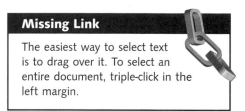

Missing Link

The easiest way to select text is to drag over it. To select an entire document, triple-click in the left margin.

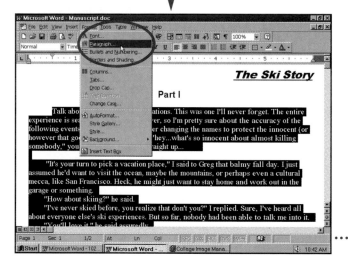

2 Open the **Format** menu and select **Paragraph**. This opens the Paragraph dialog box.

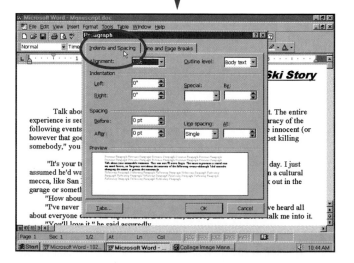

3 Click on the **Indents and Spacing** tab to bring its options to the front of the dialog box.

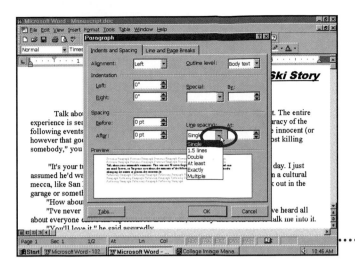

4 Click on the **Line Spacing** drop-down list in the Spacing area of the dialog box to display a list of line spacing styles.

5 Click on the line spacing style you want to use. For example, to double-space your document text, click on **Double**. The Preview area shows you what the selected line spacing will look like in your document.

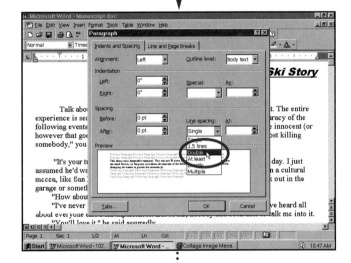

Missing Link

For a line spacing shortcut, press **Ctrl+2** to double-space the selected text. To specify single spacing, press **Ctrl+1**; for 1-1/2 lines, press **Ctrl+5**.

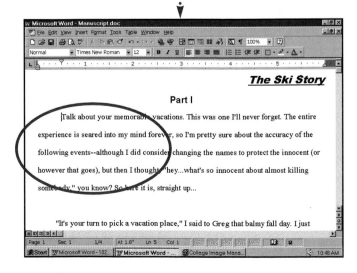

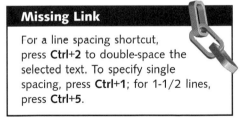

6 Click **OK** to exit the dialog box and apply the line spacing. ■

Puzzled?

To undo the line spacing change, immediately click the **Undo** button on the Standard toolbar.

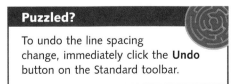

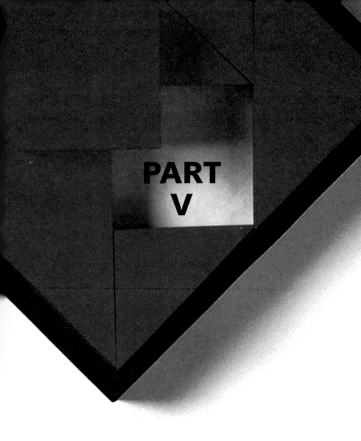

PART V

More Editing Techniques

AFTER YOU'VE CREATED A DOCUMENT and applied formatting commands, there are some additional tools you can use to check over your document. For example, did you know Word comes with a spell checking tool you can use to help edit your document for spelling errors? You can even tap into an electronic thesaurus. In this part of the book, you'll learn about several of Word's editing tools that can help you perfect your document.

When it comes to the task of searching through a document for a particular word, nothing beats Word's search features. The Find command enables you to search for specific text, character formats such as bold, italic, and underline, or paragraph formats such as indents and spacing. The text you search for can also include a special character, page breaks, section breaks, and any other special characters that appear in a document.

Not only can you find data buried in a lengthy document, you can also replace it with new text. Word's Replace feature lets you find anything the Find command does, and then change it to anything else. You can change a word or phrase, character formats, paragraph formats, or any special character throughout the document quickly and easily.

The Find and Replace commands give you several search options to refine the search:

- The Search option lets you specify the direction of the search in the document. You can choose All to search the entire document from the insertion point; Down to search forward, and Up to search backward in the document.

- The Match Case option searches for text with the specified combination of upper- and lowercase letters.

- The Find Whole Words Only search option searches for whole words only and does not find occurrences of the word that are part of other words.

- The Use Wildcards option searches for specified wildcards, special characters, or special search operators that you type into the Find what text box.

- The Sounds Like option searches for homonyms —words that sound like the current word for which you are searching.

- The Find All Word Forms option finds and replaces all forms of a word.

No word processing program would be complete these days without a spell checker. With Word's spelling feature, you can use custom dictionaries for medical, legal, and technical documents to ensure accuracy when spell-checking special terms for documents in those fields. You can start Word's spell check feature by opening the Tools menu and selecting Spelling, or you can just click on the Spelling & Grammar button on the Standard toolbar. Word automatically checks your document and points out any discrepancies in spellings. Not only that, but Word offers you a listing of other choices you can use in place of the misspelled word.

If you're not the greatest speller in the world, the AutoCorrect feature can really help you out. AutoCorrect checks your spelling as you type, automatically. Any misspellings you make are underlined with a red wavy line. To fix a mistake, just right-click over a misspelled word to summon a shortcut menu listing replacement words. It's rather like having an English teacher standing nearby! In addition to the custom dictionaries Word taps into, you can also look up words in an electronic Thesaurus. The Thesaurus is very useful for looking up synonyms and antonyms for words used in your document.

This part will introduce you to some of Word's time-saving features for editing data in your documents.

TASK 35

Searching for Text

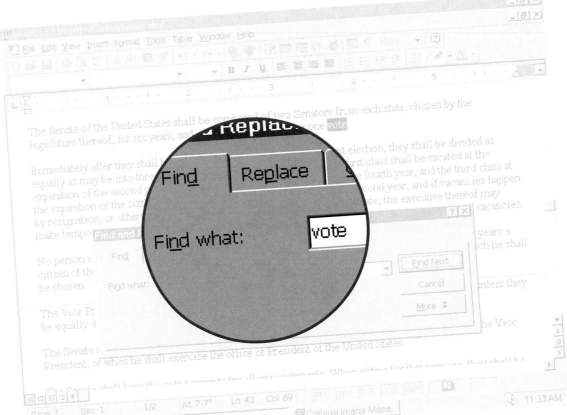

"Why would I do this?"

There's nothing more daunting than the task of searching through a long document looking for a particular word or phrase. For example, perhaps you want to re-read the paragraphs in your 12-page report covering the topic of "bio-medical technologies." Rather than slowly scroll through each page looking for the words, why not let Word 97 find the text for you?

The Find feature enables you to quickly locate a specific word or phrase, character format, paragraph format, or special character. This feature is handy when you want to find specific text in a document that is many pages long.

1 Press **Ctrl+Home**. This moves the insertion point to the beginning of the document. When you begin a search, Word searches from the location of the insertion point forward.

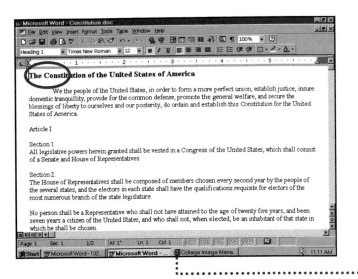

Puzzled?

Word searches from that location to the end of the document and then displays a message box that asks whether you want to continue searching from the beginning.

2 Open the **Edit** menu and select **Find**. This opens the Find and Replace dialog box onto your screen.

Missing Link

You can also click on the **Select Browse Object** button located on the vertical scroll bar (the tiny round icon sandwiched between the double-arrow buttons). This opens an icon menu from which you can select portions of the document to view. Click on the **Find** icon to open the Find and Replace dialog box.

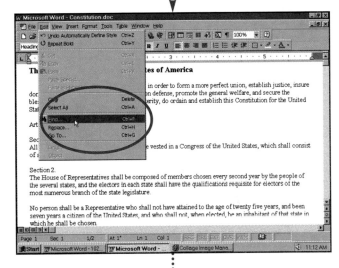

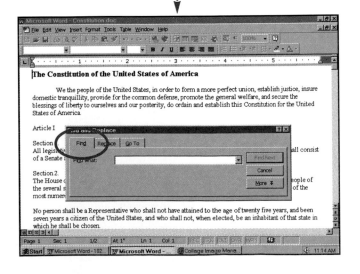

3 The Find and Replace dialog box has three tabs: Find, Replace, and Go To (you learned about using the Go To tab in Task 19). The Find tab should appear at the front of the box. If not, click on the **Find** tab name.

4 To perform a simple search, type the word or phrase you're looking for into the **Find what** text box. (The word or words you type are called the *search string*.) When you're ready to start the search, click on the **Find Next** button.

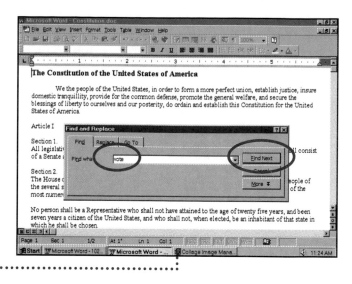

Missing Link

By default, Word finds any occurrence of this text, regardless of whether you type in upper- or lowercase characters. You can specify that you want to find only whole words and to match case. To do so, click the **More** button to display additional search options.

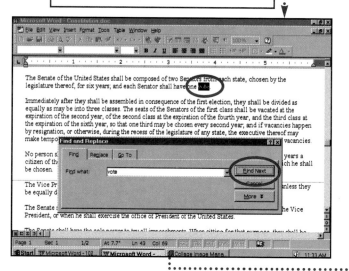

5 Word 97 finds the first occurrence of the search string and highlights that text, as shown in the example. The Find and Replace dialog box remains open on-screen. To find the next occurrence of the word or phrase, click on the **Find Next** button. If you prefer to exit the dialog box and edit the text, click on the **Cancel** button.

Puzzled?

If Word does not find the text, you see an alert message. Click **OK** and try the search again. Be sure to type the search string correctly.

6 To conduct a search using Word's search options, click on the **More** button. This expands the Find and Replace dialog box, shown in the figure, to include other search options. Select the options you want and continue with your search. If you want to search for specific formatting, click on the **Format** button. To search for special characters, click on the **Special** button. To exit the dialog box, click **Cancel.** ■

Puzzled?

Click on the **Less** button to return the Find and Replace dialog box to it's original size.

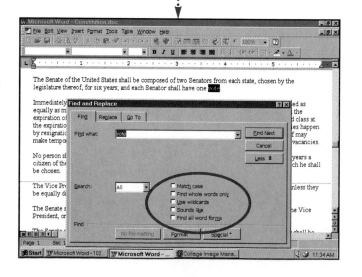

Finding and Replacing Text

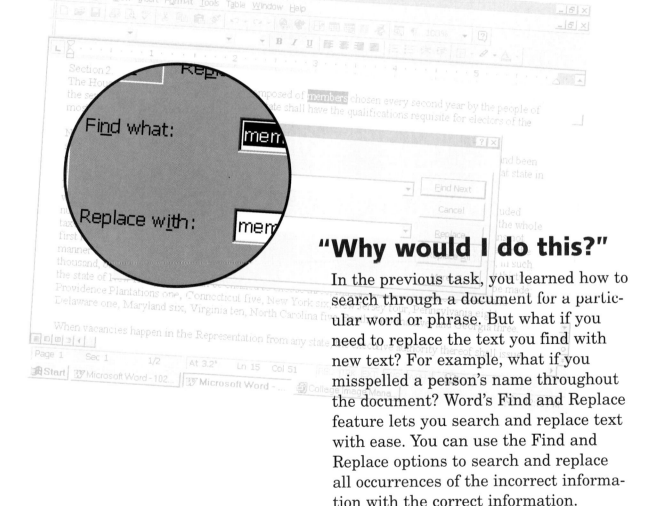

"Why would I do this?"

In the previous task, you learned how to search through a document for a particular word or phrase. But what if you need to replace the text you find with new text? For example, what if you misspelled a person's name throughout the document? Word's Find and Replace feature lets you search and replace text with ease. You can use the Find and Replace options to search and replace all occurrences of the incorrect information with the correct information.

You can locate text, character and paragraph formats, or special characters, and then replace the original text with new text.

1 Press **Ctrl+Home**. This moves the insertion point to the beginning of the document. When you begin the search, Word searches from the location of the insertion point forward.

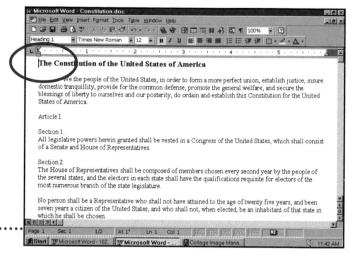

2 Open the **Edit** menu and select **Replace**. This opens the Find and Replace dialog box.

3 The Replace tab should appear at the front of the dialog box. Notice that the text from the previous search appears in the dialog box. If not, click on the **Replace** tab name.

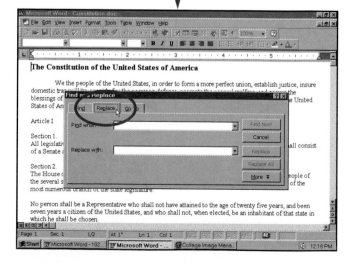

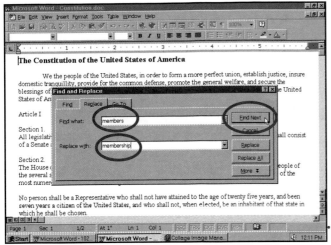

4 Type in the word or phrase you're looking for in the **Find what** text box (the text you type in is called a *search string*). Press the **Tab** key to move to the **Replace with** text box and type in the word or phrase you want to replace the original text with. Click **Find Next** to start the search.

5 Word finds the first occurrence of the search string and highlights that text in your document. To replace the highlighted text with the replacement text, click on the **Replace** button. Word automatically replaces the highlighted text with the text you specified in the **Replace with** text box. To replace all occurrences of the text in the entire document, click on the **Replace All** button. To find the next occurrence, click on the **Find Next** button.

Puzzled?

If the dialog box is in your way of viewing the document, you can move it by dragging the dialog box's title bar.

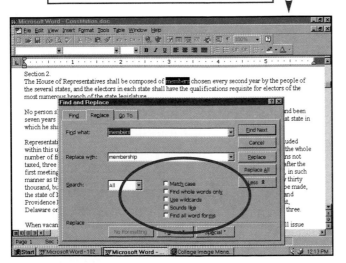

6 To use search options to help you locate the exact text you want to find and replace, click on the **More** button to expand the Find and Replace dialog box. You can now select from the options and continue the search. To search for specific formatting, click on the **Format** button. To search for special characters, click on the **Special** button. To exit the dialog box, click on **Cancel**. ■

Puzzled?

If Word does not find the text, you see an alert message. Click **OK**. Be sure to type the search string correctly.

Checking Your Spelling

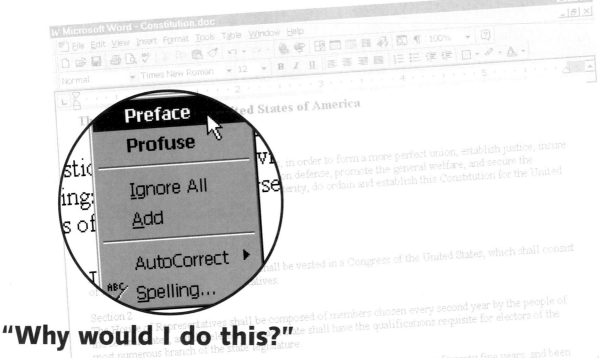

"Why would I do this?"

Word's spell checker finds and high-lights for correction the misspellings in a document. Spell-checking is an impor-tant feature that makes your documents look professional and letter perfect. The easiest way to spell check a document is to do so while you're typing it in. Word's AutoCorrect feature, which is turned on by default when you first start Word, automatically corrects misspellings as you type. You may have noticed wavy red underlines after you type in a mis-spelled word. That's the AutoCorrect feature at work.

You can also spell check a document from top to bottom with Word's spell check tool. As part of the spell check feature, Word also checks your docu-ment's grammar usage. By default, Word checks both spelling and gram-mar, but you can turn the grammar tool off and choose to check only the docu-ment's spelling errors. In this task, you'll learn how to use AutoCorrect and open the spell check tool.

1 To see how Word's AutoCorrect feature works, deliberately type in a misspelled word. For example, type in the word "Prefice." A red wavy line appears beneath the word. You'll notice the red wavy line beneath each word that contains a spelling error.

Missing Link

The AutoCorrect feature is automatically turned on by default. You can turn it off by opening the **Tools** menu. Select **Options**, then click on the **Spelling & Grammar** tab and deselect the **Check Spelling As You Type** option.

2 To correct the misspelling, move the mouse pointer to the underlined word and click the right mouse button. The Spelling shortcut menu appears. Choose a word from the suggested spelling list to change the misspelled word in the document.

Missing Link

The Spelling shortcut menu lists suggested spelling for the word not found in the dictionary. You can select from several spelling options to correct the error.

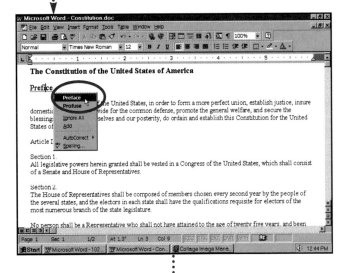

3 Word automatically corrects the misspelling with the new word you selected from the list.

Missing Link

Choose **Ignore All** from the shortcut menu to remove the red wavy underline beneath the word. The Ignore All option tells Word to ignore all occurrences of this word (that is, not to underline this specific word again).

4 You can also use Word's spell check tool to go over a document and check both spelling and grammar. For example, you may need to spell check a Word file someone else have given you, or perhaps you need to spell check a document you found on the World Wide Web before distributing it by e-mail. Click the insertion point where you want the spell check to start, then click on the **Spelling and Grammar** button on the Standard toolbar.

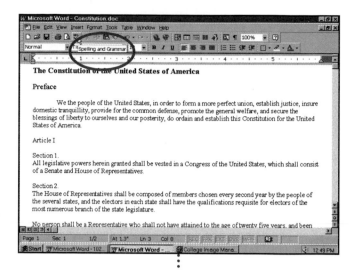

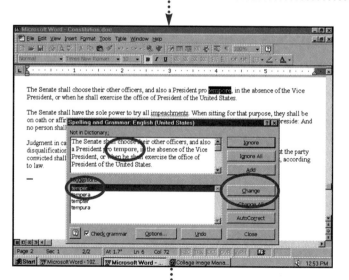

5 Word starts the spelling and grammar check. Any misspellings it comes across are highlighted in the text as well as in the Spelling and Grammar dialog box that appears on-screen. Any grammatical errors are also highlighted. The Suggestions box lists possible word or grammar suggestions you can use. To select a suggestion from the list, click on the **Change** button. Word's built-in dictionary is not comprehensive, so you may not always agree with Word's suggestions. If not, click on the **Ignore** button to continue.

6 When the spell check is complete, a dialog box appears telling you so. Click **OK**. ■

Missing Link

If Word's AutoCorrect feature becomes too annoying for you, you can turn it off. Open the **Tools** menu, select **Options**. Click on the **Spelling & Grammar** tab in the Options dialog box and de-select the **Check spelling as you type** box. Click **OK** to exit the dialog box.

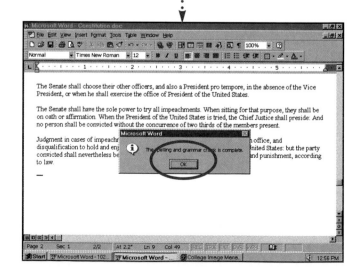

Using the Thesaurus

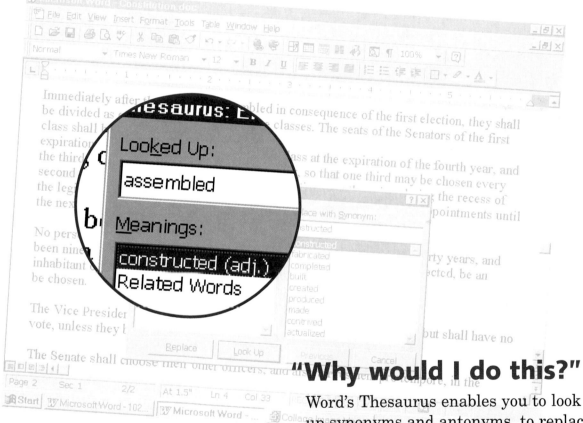

"Why would I do this?"

Word's Thesaurus enables you to look up synonyms and antonyms, to replace your words with more interesting ones, without leaving the document. You might want to use the Thesaurus to find a more common word that means the same thing so your reader can understand what you've written in the document. You might also use the Thesaurus when you find yourself using the same word over and over and need to vary your text.

1 On your document page, click within the word you want to look up or select the entire word.

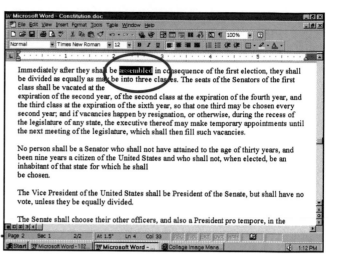

2 Open the **Tools** menu, select **Language**, then select **Thesaurus**. This opens the Thesaurus dialog box.

Missing Link

To see additional synonyms, select a synonym in the **Replace with Synonym** list, then click on the **Look Up** button to view a list of different synonyms.

3 The **Looked Up** text box displays the selected word; beneath this box, you see a list of meanings. To the right of the Looked Up box, you see a list of synonyms. Select the synonym you want to use, then click on the **Replace** button. Word replaces the text and closes the dialog box. ■

Puzzle

To undo the replacement, click the **Undo** button on the Standard toolbar immediately.

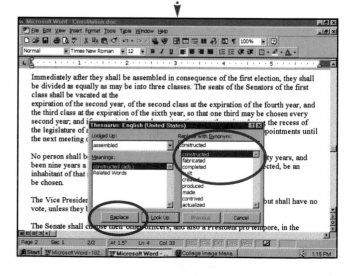

Inserting the Date

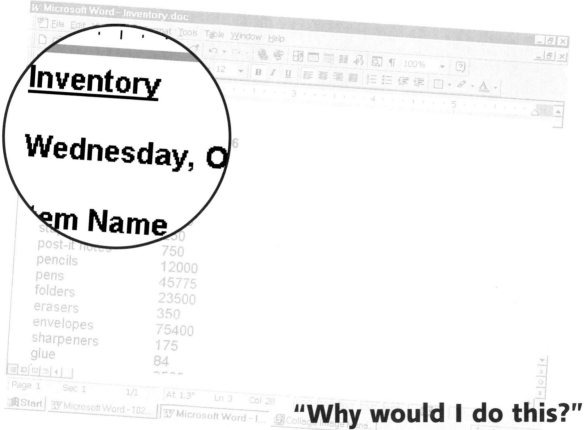

"Why would I do this?"

You can use the Date and Time command to automatically insert the date or time into a document. Adding dates to a document helps you keep track of the last time your document was modified, and it also keeps you from having to manually add this information to the document. Follow the steps in this task to insert the current date and time into your own document.

Task 39: Inserting the Date

1 With a click of your mouse button, place the insertion point where you want the date to appear. Open the **Insert** menu and select Date and Time. This opens the **Date and Time** dialog box, which lists the available date and time formats.

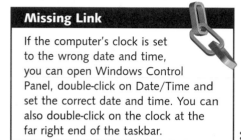

Missing Link

If the computer's clock is set to the wrong date and time, you can open Windows Control Panel, double-click on Date/Time and set the correct date and time. You can also double-click on the clock at the far right end of the taskbar.

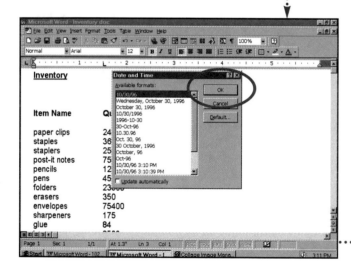

2 From the list of **Available Formats**, select the format you want to use. Click **OK** to exit the Date and Time dialog box.

3 Word inserts the date and time into the document. ■

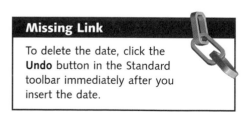

Missing Link

To delete the date, click the **Undo** button in the Standard toolbar immediately after you insert the date.

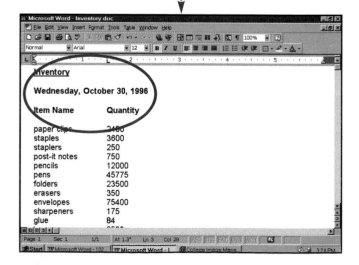

Inserting a Special Character

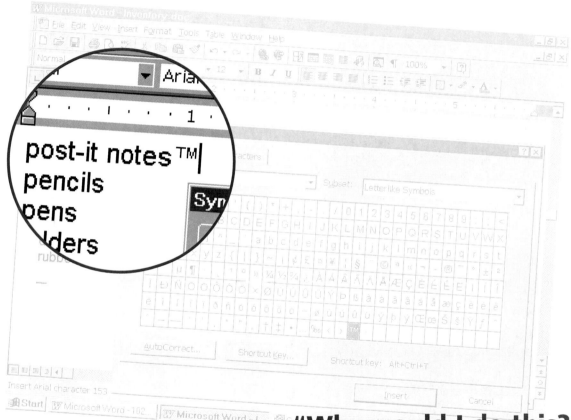

"Why would I do this?"

While checking over your document, you may notice places where you need to insert a special character. For example, you might want to insert a copyright symbol, a registered trademark symbol, or foreign language symbols in your document. Using Word's Symbol dialog box, you can insert many types of special characters in your document.

1 Click the insertion point where you want a special character added. Open the **Insert** menu and select **Symbol**. This opens the Symbol dialog box.

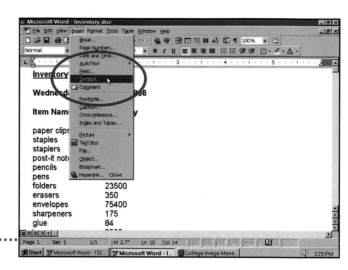

2 The Symbol dialog box has two tabs, one for symbols and one for special characters. By default, the Symbols tab appears in front. (If it doesn't, click on the **Symbols** tab.)

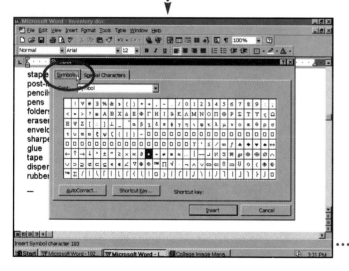

3 If you're looking for a particular symbol, look through the symbols displayed on the Symbols tab. The symbols are difficult to read, however, you can click on a symbol to enlarge it. When you find the symbol you want, select it, then click on the **Insert** button and it's added to your document (see Step 6). If you've finished, click on the **Close** button to close the Symbol dialog box.

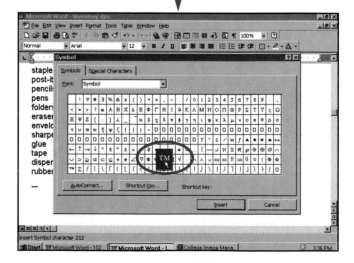

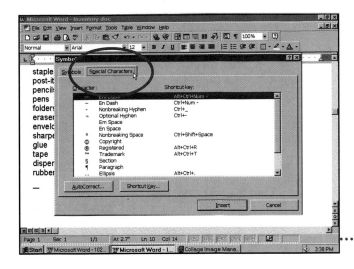

4 To insert a special character at the insertion point, click on the **Special Characters** tab name to bring the options to the front of the Symbol dialog box.

5 Click on the special character you want to insert, then click on the **Insert** button. Click on the **Close** button to close the dialog box.

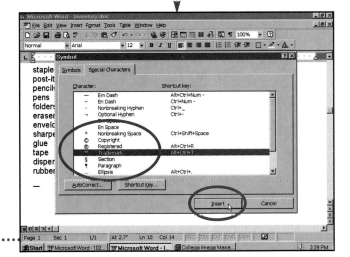

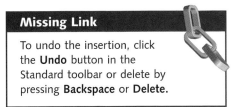

6 The selected symbol or special character now appears in your document. ■

Missing Link

To undo the insertion, click the **Undo** button in the Standard toolbar or delete by pressing **Backspace** or **Delete**.

PART VI

More Formatting

▲ ● ■ ● ■ ▲ ● ■ ▲ ●

N THIS PART, YOU LEARN HOW TO add some additional formatting to your documents, including how to place a border around a paragraph, shade a paragraph, center a page, number pages, and create and edit headers and footers.

Adding borders to your text is a great way of setting apart important information or creating a unique look for titles and headings. You can use the Borders button on the Formatting toolbar to add boxes around paragraphs, and add emphasis lines anywhere in the document. Adding a border and lines helps distinguish document headings or sections. Adding lines works well on newsletters, for example. Lines can also be used to separate parts of a document. The Sample Documents section (Part X) contains several documents that show off these features.

Not only can you add boxes around your text, you can also shade the boxes, giving your document background more depth and visual style. Pull down the Format menu and select Borders and Shading to open the Borders and Shading dialog box, where you'll find shading controls along with border options. The dialog box has a variety of controls for creating just the right border around your text.

Another way to control the positioning of text in your document is with vertical alignment. When you choose the File, Page Setup command, you see the Page Setup dialog box. The Layout options in the Page Setup dialog box include options for sections, headers and footers, vertical alignment, and line numbers. In this part, you learn how to center a page vertically with the vertical alignment option. It is a good idea to experiment with all the layout options until you get the results you want.

When you start creating long documents consisting of many pages, you'll want to add page numbers to help keep the documents organized, particularly if you print them out and give them to someone else to read. When you add page numbers with the Insert, Page Numbers command, you add them to a header or footer. You can specify whether to add the page numbers to the top of each page (to a header) or to the bottom of each page (to a footer). You can also specify the alignment.

If you want, you can change the format for the page numbers. Click the Format button in the Page Numbers dialog box and Word displays the Page Number Format dialog box. From the Number Format list, you can select Arabic numerals (1,2,3 . . .), which is the default, lowercase or uppercase letters, or lowercase or uppercase Roman numerals.

Word lets you add headers and footers to print information other than page numbers at the top and bottom of every page of the printout. For example, you might add a header to the top of every page that includes your company name, your name, and the date. You can create your own header and footer information, and you can include any text plus special commands to control the appearance of the header or footer.

If you have a document that is divided into multiple sections, you can define individual headers and footers for each section. Word also lets you create different headers or footers for odd and even pages, and for the first page in a document or section. To do so, choose the File, Page Setup command and click the Layout tab. Then you can choose the Headers and Footers options you want.

This part shows you how to apply each of the formatting operations described on these two pages.

Adding a Border to a Paragraph

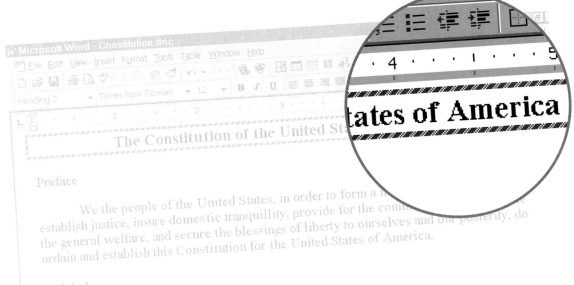

"Why would I do this?"

To really set off your text, try adding a border around it. With Word's Borders and Shading options you can add boxes around your text. For example, you can place single or double-lined boxes around a title to create a professional-looking cover page. Or you can add a double underline on the bottom of each heading in your report to make the sections stand out.

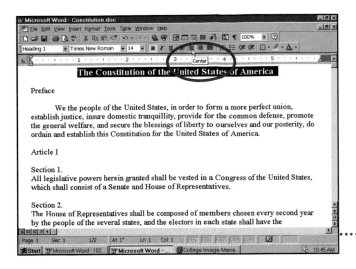

1 Select the paragraph you want to place a border around. For maximum effect, center the text.

2 Click the **Outside Border** button (the button with a thick border and four squares inside the border) on the Formatting toolbar. Immediately, Word adds a default border around the selected paragraph.

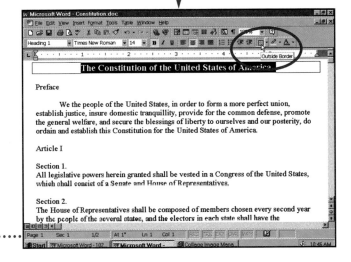

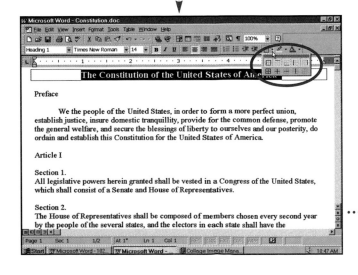

3 Click the down arrow next to the **Borders** button on the Formatting toolbar to display a table of border edge styles. With the Borders drop-down table, you can add lines at the top, bottom, left, or right side of your paragraph. You can select a style from this list by clicking on its button.

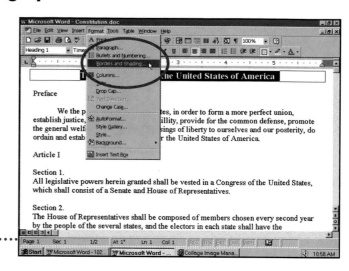

4 If you're looking for more border options than those found with the Borders button, you need to open the Borders and Shading dialog box. Select the text you want to add a border for, then pull down the **Format** menu and select **Borders and Shading**.

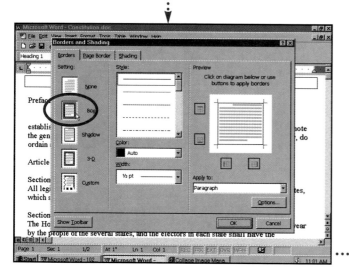

5 In the Borders tab, you'll find all kinds of options for creating borders. Under the **Setting** area, select a border to use.

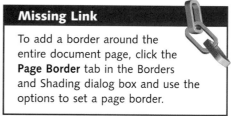

Missing Link

To add a border around the entire document page, click the **Page Border** tab in the Borders and Shading dialog box and use the options to set a page border.

6 In the **Style** list box you can select a specific line style to use. Scroll down the list and click the line style you want to apply.

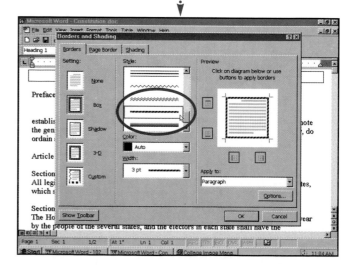

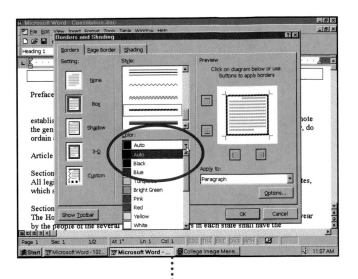

7 To change the border's color, use the **Color** drop-down list and select a color to use.

Missing Link

If you prefer to work with the border options outside of the Borders and Shading dialog box, you can click the **Show Toolbar** button in the Borders and Shading dialog box, and a floating Tables and Borders toolbar appears on-screen. Use the buttons on the floating toolbar to change the appearance of your border. To close the toolbar, click it's **Close** button.

8 To see how the border will look on your document page, look at the **Preview** area.

Missing Link

To control how precisely the border fits around the text, click the **Options** button in the Borders and Shading dialog box to display options for setting exact dimensions.

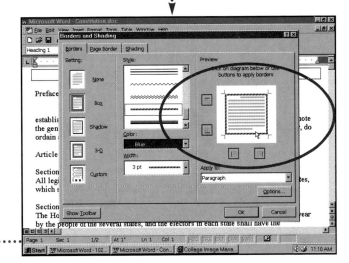

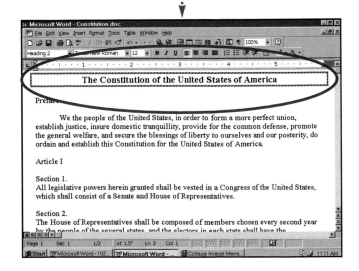

9 If you're happy with your selections, click the **OK** button to exit the dialog box and apply the border styles to the paragraph you selected. ■

Puzzled?

To remove the border, immediately click the **Undo** button on the Standard toolbar.

TASK 42

Shading A Paragraph

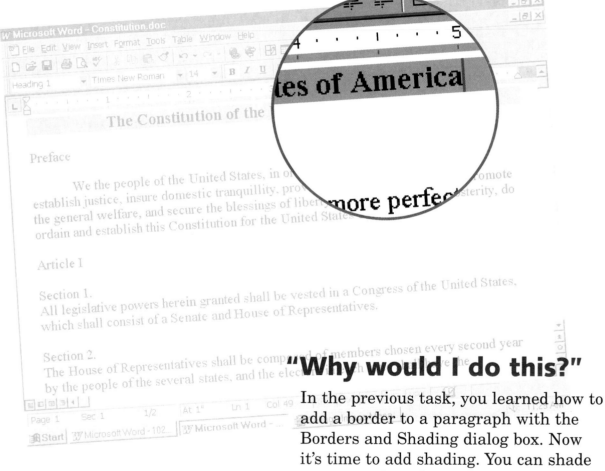

"Why would I do this?"

In the previous task, you learned how to add a border to a paragraph with the Borders and Shading dialog box. Now it's time to add shading. You can shade a paragraph to draw attention to certain text in your document. You might want to shade a title, a quotation, or a note surrounded with a border. You don't have to add a border in order to add shading. The shading command simply adds a shaded background behind your text.

1 Select the paragraph you want to add shading to.

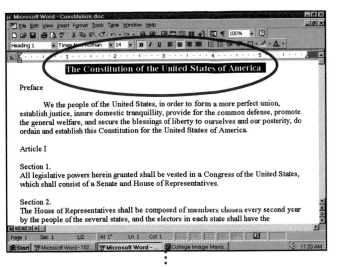

2 Open the **Format** menu and select **Borders and Shading**. This opens the Borders and Shading dialog box.

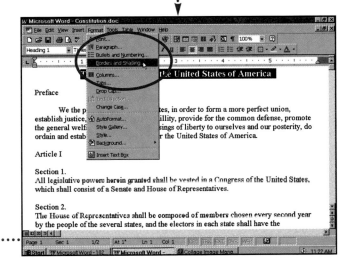

3 Click the **Shading** tab to bring it to the front of the dialog box. The Shading tab has options for creating a shading fill and shading patterns.

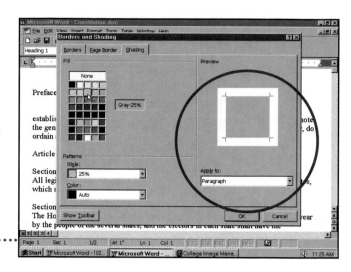

4 Select a shading fill from the **Fill** table. Look over at the **Preview** area to see what the shading fill will look like in the document.

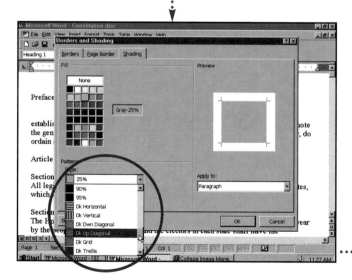

5 To select a pattern to use as your shading, click the **Style** drop-down list and scroll through the list to select a pattern. To choose a color for the shading, use the **Color** drop-down list.

6 To apply your shading options, click the **OK** button. The shading is added to the selected paragraph in the document. ■

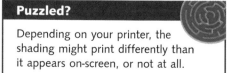

Puzzled?

Depending on your printer, the shading might print differently than it appears on-screen, or not at all.

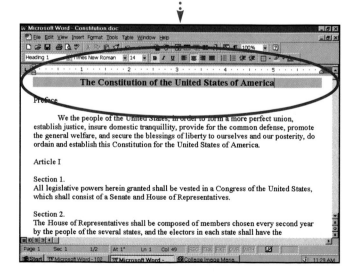

Centering a Page Vertically

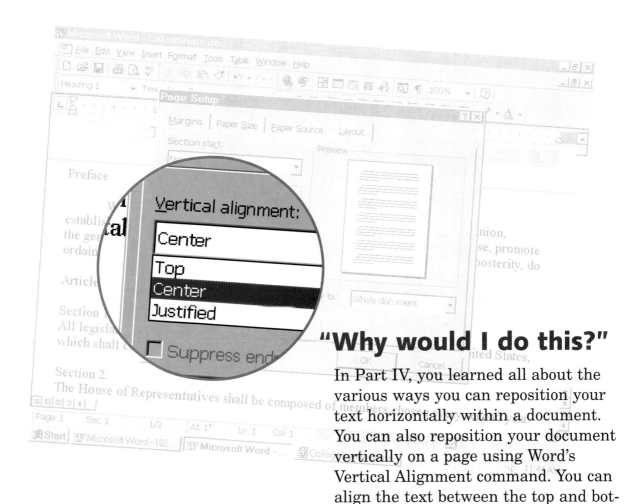

"Why would I do this?"

In Part IV, you learned all about the various ways you can reposition your text horizontally within a document. You can also reposition your document vertically on a page using Word's Vertical Alignment command. You can align the text between the top and bottom margins. Centering a page works well for special documents, such as an invitation. Letters often look better on the page when they are centered. Document, chapter, or report titles look better on a title page when they are centered.

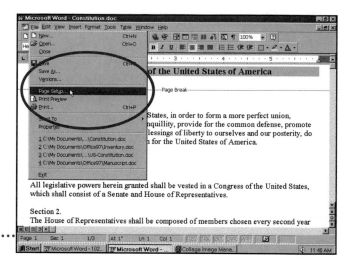

1 Press **Ctrl+Home** or scroll to the top of the document, then open the **File** menu and select **Page Setup**. This opens the Page Setup dialog box.

2 Click the **Layout** tab to display the Layout options. Click the **Vertical Alignment** down arrow to display a drop-down list of alignment choices. Select **Center** from the list.

3 Click **OK** to close the Page Setup dialog box and apply the new alignment. You won't be able to see the vertical alignment change on-screen. To see how things look, click the **Print Preview** button (the button with a piece of paper and magnifying glass). After viewing the document, click the **Close** button in the Preview Window to close it. ■

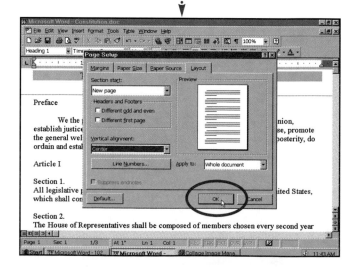

Numbering Pages

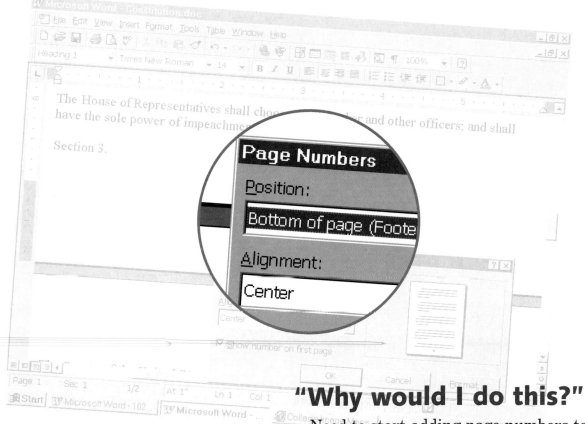

"Why would I do this?"

Need to start adding page numbers to your lengthy document? Word has a page numbering feature that automatically inserts page numbers and prints the page numbers in the position you specify. That way, you don't have to manually enter and manage the page numbers. Page numbering is often used on manuscript pages or reports.

Task 44: Numbering Pages

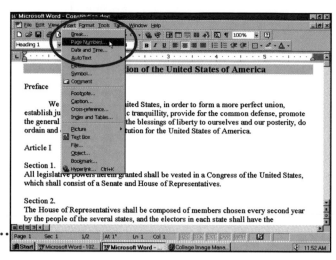

1 To insert page numbers, open the **Insert** menu and select the **Page Numbers** command. This opens the Page Numbers dialog box.

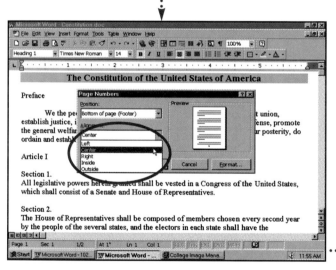

2 To change the page number position, such as top or bottom of the page, click the **Position** drop-down arrow and select a position from the list. To change the page number alignment, click the **Alignment** drop-down arrow to display a list of alignment choices. Make a selection from the list.

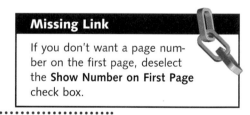

Missing Link

If you don't want a page number on the first page, deselect the **Show Number on First Page** check box.

3 Look in the **Preview** box to see how the numbers will appear on the document page. Click **OK** to exit the dialog box and add page numbers to your document. On-screen, you cannot see the page numbers unless you switch over to Page Layout view (open the View menu and select Page Layout). ■

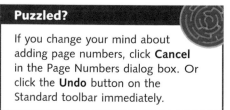

Puzzled?

If you change your mind about adding page numbers, click **Cancel** in the Page Numbers dialog box. Or click the **Undo** button on the Standard toolbar immediately.

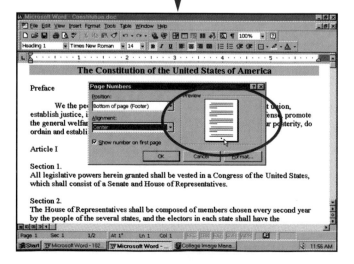

Creating and Editing Headers and Footers

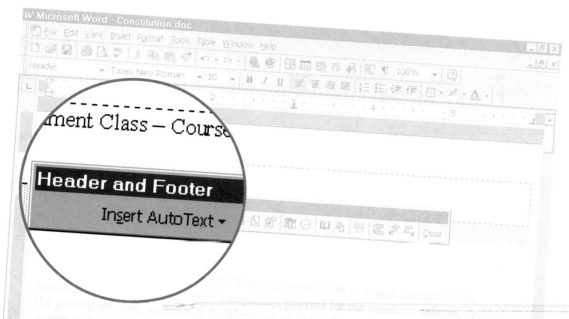

"Why would I do this?"

Headers and footers are lines of text that you can print at the top and bottom of every page in a print job—headers at the top, footers at the bottom. You can include any text, page numbers, the current date and time, and even format the information in a header and footer. For example, if you're creating a business report, you might add a header or footer containing the company name, your name, and the date the report was created.

Headers and footers will appear on every page, unless you specify otherwise. You can use the Page Setup dialog box to tell Word to print headers or footers on every page, even or odd pages. You can even tell Word to start headers and footers on a different start page. Click the **Page Setup** button on the Header and Footer toolbar to control how headers and footers print.

Task 45: Creating and Editing Headers and Footers

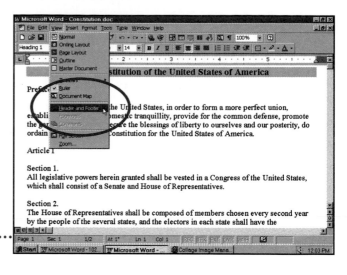

1 Open the **View** menu and select **Header and Footer**. This displays the Header and Footer areas on-screen. You also see the Header and Footer toolbar.

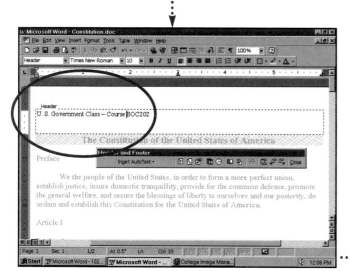

2 By default, Word starts you out ready to add a header. To enter header text, just start typing.

Puzzled?

If the Header and Footer floating toolbar is in your way, you can move it by dragging its title bar.

3 Use the Header and Footer floating toolbar to add things like the date and time to your header or footer. For example, to add the date to your header, click the **Insert Date** button on the toolbar.

Puzzled?

If you're not sure about using the Header and Footer toolbar buttons, there's an easy way you can learn what each button does. Hover your mouse pointer over a toolbar button to display the ScreenTip name.

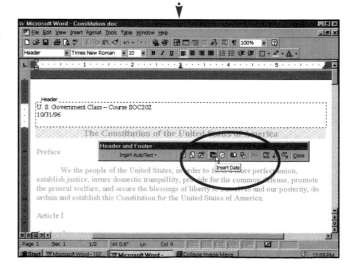

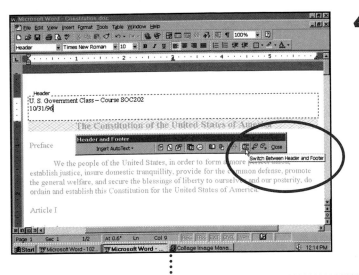

4 To add a footer to your document, click the **Switch Between Header and Footer** button. This button lets you move back and forth from the top to the bottom of the page.

Missing Link

Word 97 has added a handy new feature to the Header and Footer toolbar. Click the **Insert AutoText** button to add commonly-used header and footer text to your documents, such as the *filename* and *created by*, just to name a few.

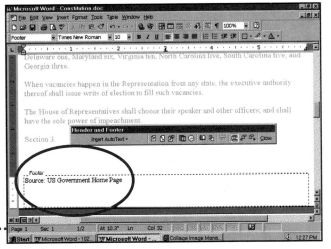

5 To start adding footer text, simply start typing. Use the Header and Footer toolbar buttons to add other items to your footer, such as the time or page numbers.

6 When finished working with headers and footers, click **Close** in the Header and Footer toolbar. This step confirms the header and footer and closes the Header window. On-screen, you cannot see the header and footer. To do so, you must preview the document or switch to Page Layout view (open the **View** menu and select **Page Layout**). ■

Puzzled?

If you don't want a header or footer, select all the text in the Header or Footer area and then press **Delete** to delete the header or footer.

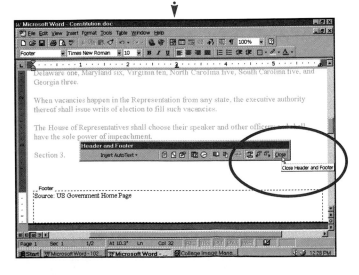

PART VII

Enhancing Your Document

AFTER YOU'VE GAINED SOME EXPERIENCE using Word 97, you may want to start adding items into your documents to enhance the presentation of data. For example, you might want to add a graphic to your report, or add the company logo to your letters and faxes. Or maybe you want to turn a boring list into a table. Enhancing your documents is easy in Word and this part of the book will show you how.

In this section, you will learn how to insert a graphic, move and resize a graphic, and delete a graphic. You'll also learn how to create and work with Word tables, including how to enter text in a table, add a row to a table, and delete a column from a table. You will learn how to create a two-column document, type text into a two-column document, and insert a WordArt object. And for those of you that have color printers, you will learn how add color to your text.

Adding graphics is a great way to spice up your document. Word 97 comes with some clip-art files you can use. You can insert a graphic image that you create with Word's Drawing features or a graphic from another program. Word supports many import file types and various graphics formats, so you can easily insert graphics from other programs.

Word's Drawing feature lets you create your own graphics. For example, with Word's AutoShapes feature, you can add shapes to your documents, such as arrows, starbursts, and balloons. When you insert a graphic into your document, Word treats the graphic as an object you can move and resize. You can select the graphic and then move it to a new location in your document, or stretch/shrink the graphics to any shape and size you want. If you no longer want the graphic in your document, you can delete the graphic.

Tables are another way of adding visual interest to a page. The Table feature enables you to create a table with columns and rows, instantly. Then, you can enter text and numbers (similar to a spreadsheet) in the table without defining tab settings. Once you create the table, you can easily insert and delete rows in the table to suit your needs.

There are several other things you can do to customize a table. You can join cells, split cells, and hide or show gridlines in a table. You can even sort text and numbers in a table, create formulas to perform math calculations on numbers in a table, and import a spreadsheet file into a table.

Why confine your text to a one-column format? You can create a two-column document, which looks like newspaper-style columns. Newspaper-style columns are sometimes referred to as snaking columns. Snaking columns contain text that wraps from the bottom of one column to the top of the next column. Two-column documents are handy for newspapers, newsletters, bulletins, magazine articles, lists, and indexes.

Once you create the two-column document, you can start entering text into the two columns. As you type the text, Word wraps the text within the column until you reach the bottom of the page and then wraps it to the top of the next column.

The Format Columns command enables you to change the column definition of your columns. For example, you can change the number of columns, the space between columns, the width of the columns, and other options in the Columns dialog box.

You can also move around columns with the cursor movement keys, as well as copy, move, and delete columns.

This part shows you enhancement techniques available to embellish your documents.

Inserting a Graphic

"Why would I do this?"

You're not limited to using just text in your Word documents. You can also insert graphics. Graphics can add emphasis and visual impact, as well as liven up any document. Once you've added a graphic, you can move it, resize it, and even make changes to its color and background.

You can choose to insert graphics from other programs or files, or you can use pictures from Word's own clip-art files. When you save your document, the graphic is saved along with the Word 97 file.

1 Place the insertion point where you want to insert a graphic. (Remember, after adding the graphic, you can always move it to a new location.) Click the **Page Layout** view button (located to the left of the horizontal scroll bar). The button is shown in the figure.

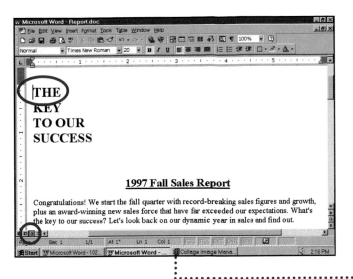

> **Puzzled?**
>
> In order to view graphics on the document page, you must use Page Layout view. To learn more about Word view options, turn to Task 54 in Part VIII.

2 Open the **Insert** menu and select **Picture**. This opens a submenu from which you can select the type of graphic you want to insert. To use a clip-art picture, click the **From File** option.

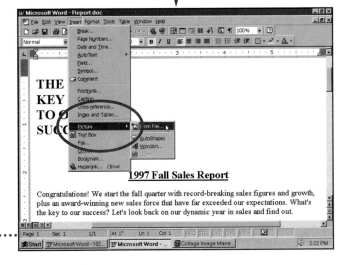

3 The Insert Picture dialog box opens. From here you can locate the clip-art file you want to use and preview pictures before making a selection. Use the Look in box to locate the folder containing the clip-art you want to use.

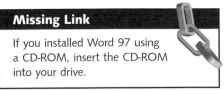

> **Missing Link**
>
> If you installed Word 97 using a CD-ROM, insert the CD-ROM into your drive.

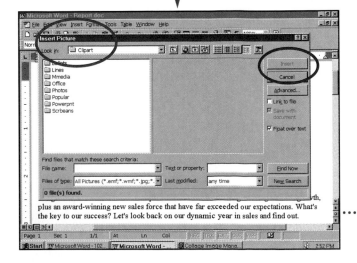

4 When you locate the exact picture file you want to use, click the file name to preview the picture. To use the picture in your Word document, select the file name and click the **Insert** button.

Puzzled?

If the Preview area isn't displayed in your dialog box, click the **Preview** button in the Insert Picture toolbar.

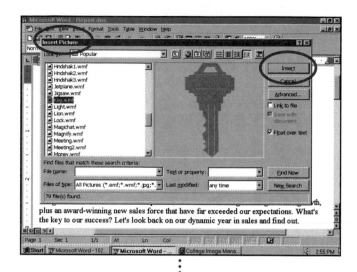

5 After clicking the **Insert** button, Word returns to the document page and inserts the graphic on-screen. Click the graphic, and you'll see tiny boxes surrounding the object. Those are called *selection handles*. When a graphic object is selected, a floating Picture toolbar appears on-screen. The toolbar has buttons for manipulating the graphic.

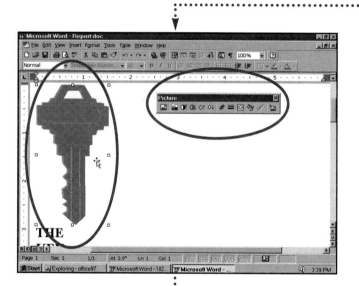

Missing Link

If the Picture toolbar is in your way, you can move it elsewhere on your screen. Simply drag it to a new location by its title bar.

6 To resize a graphic, use the selection handles to drag the object to a new shape. Depending on how you want the object resized, you'll need to drag the appropriate handle. For example, if you drag a handle on the right side of an object, the pointer takes the shape of a double-sided arrow. If you drag a corner handle, the entire object is resized.

Puzzled?

If your Picture toolbar is missing, right-click the graphic object and select **Show Picture Toolbar** from the shortcut menu.

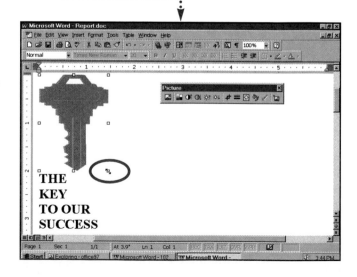

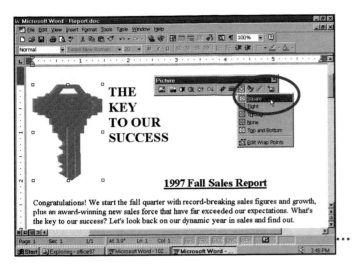

7 If you want text to surround the graphic, click the **Text Wrapping** button on the Picture toolbar. This displays a list of text wrapping options. Text wrapping is how the text flows around the graphic object. In the example shown, I chose **Square Wrapping** to bring the existing text up next to the graphic object.

8 To edit a graphic's colors or background, click the **Format Picture** button on the Picture toolbar. This opens the Format Picture dialog box.

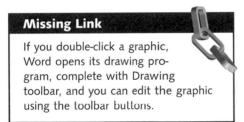

Missing Link

If you double-click a graphic, Word opens its drawing program, complete with Drawing toolbar, and you can edit the graphic using the toolbar buttons.

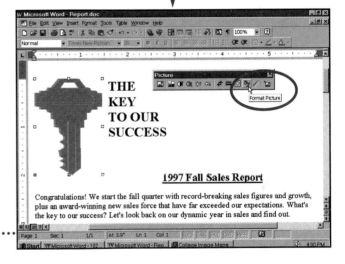

9 You can select from a variety of formatting tabs, and use the options to change the appearance and positioning of the object. For example, click the **Colors and Lines** tab and use the options to set a new background color, called a *Fill*, which changes the line style around the graphic. Click **OK** to exit the dialog box and apply the changes. ■

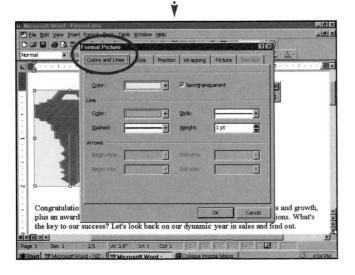

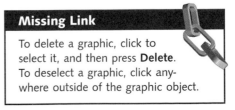

Missing Link

To delete a graphic, click to select it, and then press **Delete**. To deselect a graphic, click anywhere outside of the graphic object.

Adding Shapes

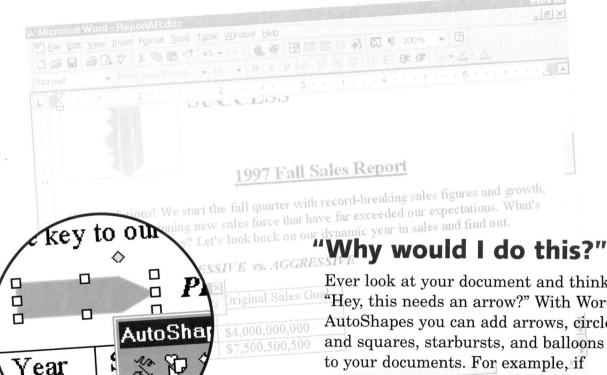

"Why would I do this?"

Ever look at your document and think, "Hey, this needs an arrow?" With Word's AutoShapes you can add arrows, circles and squares, starbursts, and balloons to your documents. For example, if you're creating a flowchart depicting your company's manufacturing process, you might want to insert some arrows to help the reader visualize the data.

Once you've added a shape, you can edit it to suit your needs. You can fill it in with color, change its line style, even rotate the shape to point in another direction. You can do all of these things using Word's Drawing toolbar.

In this task, you'll learn how to add a shape and work with some of the tools on the Drawing toolbar.

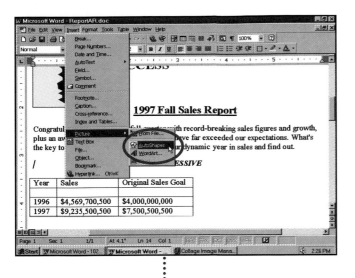

1 To insert a shape into your document, first open the **Insert** menu, select **Picture**, then **AutoShapes**. The AutoShapes floating toolbar appears on-screen and the Drawing toolbar appears at the bottom of the Word screen.

Puzzled?

To move the AutoShapes floating toolbar out of the way, drag its title bar to a new location on-screen.

2 To select a shape from the AutoShapes floating toolbar, click the category button you want to use to display a list table of shapes. Click the shape you want to draw.

Missing Link

The Drawing toolbar also has an option for selecting AutoShapes. Unlike the AutoShapes floating toolbar, when you select the AutoShapes button on the Drawing toolbar, the shapes appear as a list anchored to the Drawing toolbar.

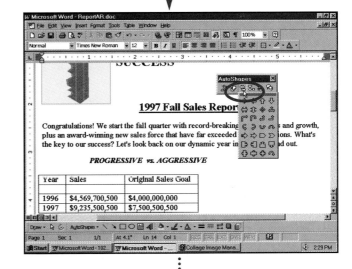

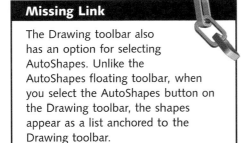

3 Move your mouse pointer to the area where you want to draw the shape. Hold down the left mouse button, and drag the pointer to the desired shape size. When you release the button, the shape appears. When selected, it appears surrounded with tiny boxes, called *selection handles*. Drag a handle to resize the object.

Missing Link

To move a shape, select it, then point to the middle of the object so the pointer takes the shape of a four-sided arrow. Drag the object to a new location and release the mouse button.

4 To fill the shape with color, click the **Fill Color** drop-down arrow on the Drawing toolbar. This displays a color palette from which you can select a specific color. Click the one you want and the shape is filled with the color.

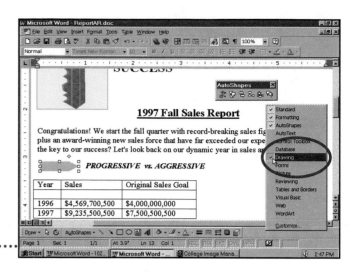

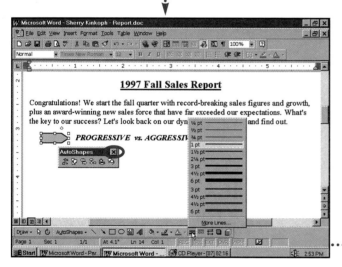

5 To change the Shapes line style, click the **Line Style** button on the Drawing toolbar. This opens a list of line styles. Click the one you want to use. When finished creating and editing a shape, close the Auto-Shapes floating toolbar by clicking its **Close** button.

6 To close the Drawing toolbar, right-click anywhere on the toolbar and deselect **Drawing** on the toolbar menu list. To close the AutoShapes toolbar, click its **Close** button. ■

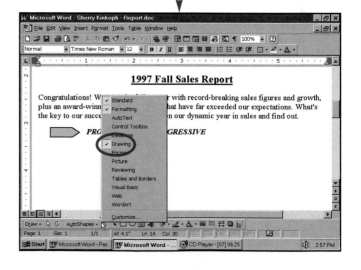

Missing Link

In order to see the shapes you've added to the document, you must be in Page Layout view. Learn more about Word view options in Task 54 in Part VIII.

Creating a Table

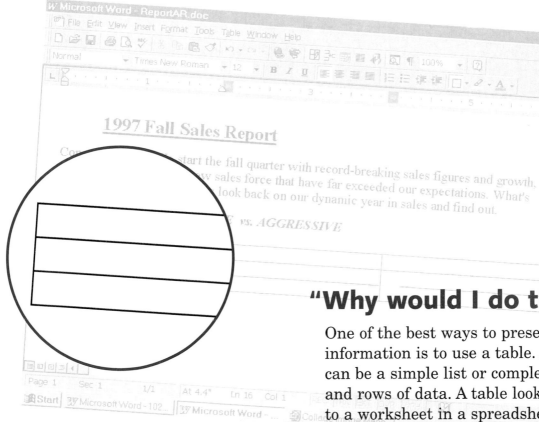

"Why would I do this?"

One of the best ways to present ordered information is to use a table. A table can be a simple list or complex columns and rows of data. A table looks similar to a worksheet in a spreadsheet program. You might want to create a table for an annual report or a sales report.

Tables are easier to work with than tabs if you have to set a grid of information (columns and rows). You organize items by columns and rows without calculating tab settings. You can even add borders and lines to your tables to make them even more appealing.

1 Move the insertion point to the area of the document where you want to insert a table. Click the **Insert Table** button on the Standard toolbar. Word displays a grid below the Insert Table button.

Missing Link

Convert text into a table by using tabs to separate columns and paragraph marks that indicate the end of rows. Select the text and choose Table, Convert Text to Table and select the options you want.

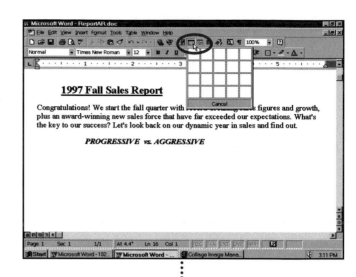

2 Highlight the exact number of columns and rows you want to use by moving your mouse over the appropriate number of column and row blocks on the grid. For example, to create a table with 3 columns and 3 rows, highlight the first three columns and first three rows on the grid. Once you've highlighted the size of your table, click the last row or column in the highlighted group.

Puzzled?

You can always add or delete rows later (see Task 50).

3 Word inserts a table with three columns and three rows on-screen. If you decide not to use the table, click the **Undo** button. ■

Missing Link

If you prefer to use a dialog box, open the Table menu and select the Insert Table command. This opens a dialog box where you can specify the number of columns and rows numerically.

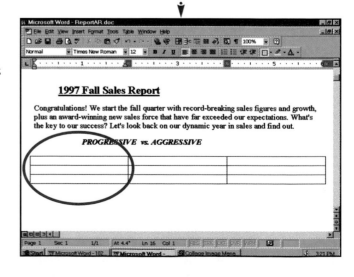

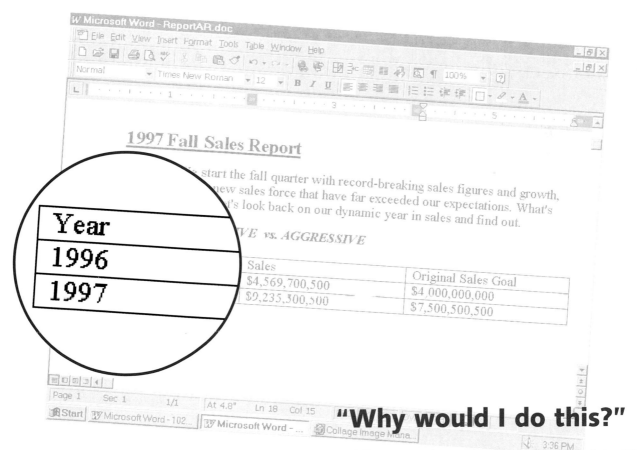

Entering Text in a Table

"Why would I do this?"

After creating a table, you'll want to fill it with text. A Word table contains columns and rows and looks similar to a spreadsheet. The intersection of a row and a column in the table is called a *cell*. You can enter text into a cell in the table by clicking inside the cell, typing the text, and pressing Tab to move to the next cell.

1 Click inside the first cell to place the insertion point, if it's not there already. Type in your text.

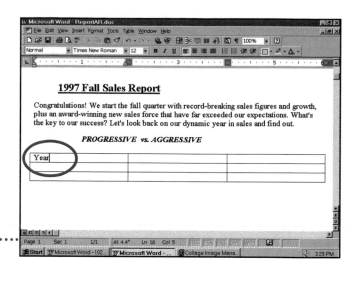

2 When you're ready to move to the next cell, you don't have to click inside it. Just press the **Tab** key on the keyboard. This moves the insertion point to the next column in that row.

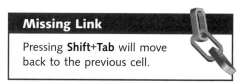

Missing Link

Pressing **Shift+Tab** will move back to the previous cell.

3 Continue entering text and pressing **Tab** to move from cell to cell until the entire table is filled. ■

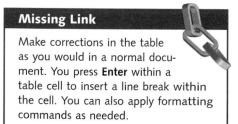

Missing Link

Make corrections in the table as you would in a normal document. You press **Enter** within a table cell to insert a line break within the cell. You can also apply formatting commands as needed.

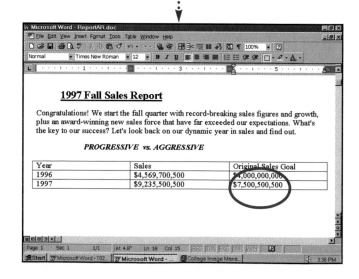

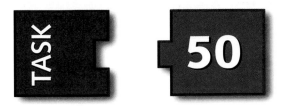

Adding and Deleting Rows and Columns in a Table

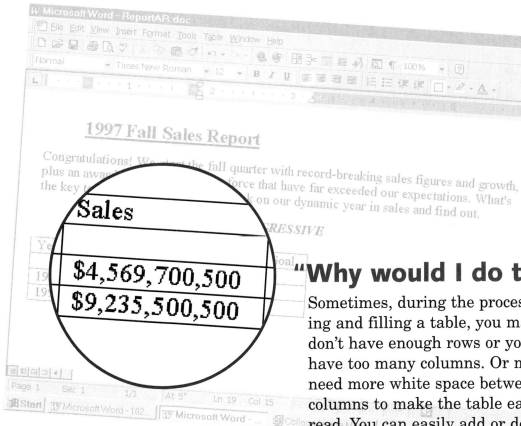

"Why would I do this?"

Sometimes, during the process of creating and filling a table, you may find you don't have enough rows or you may have too many columns. Or maybe you need more white space between rows or columns to make the table easier to read. You can easily add or delete rows and columns in your table. You can insert a row or column in a table to add additional text or spacing. You might want to delete a row or rows that you no longer want from a table, or you may want to close up some empty space.

1 To add a row, first put the insertion point where you want to insert the row.

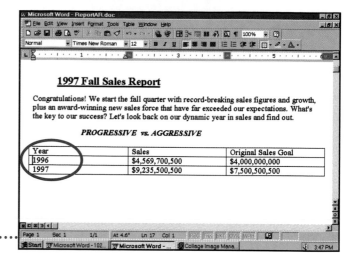

2 Open the **Table** menu and click **Insert Rows**.

Missing Link

As a shortcut, you can put the insertion point in the cell of the last row and column of the table and press **Tab** to create a new row.

3 A row is inserted in the table.

Puzzled?

To undo a change made to your table, click the **Undo** button on the Standard toolbar.

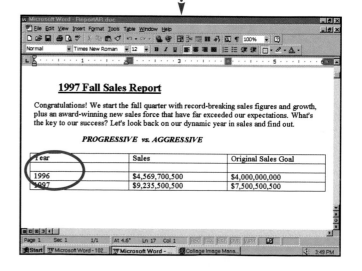

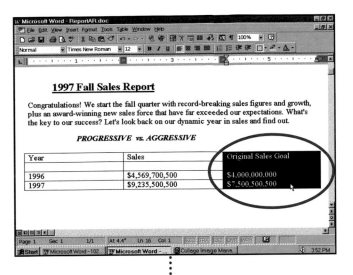

4 To insert a new column, first select the column to the right of where you want the new column inserted.

5 Open the **Table** menu and select **Insert Columns**.

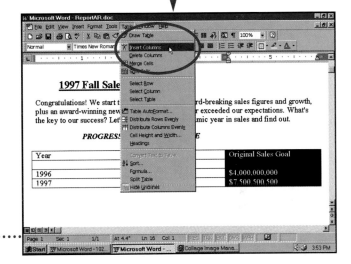

6 Word inserts the new column into your table.

7 To delete a row or column, first select the entire row or column, then click the **Cut** button on the Standard toolbar.

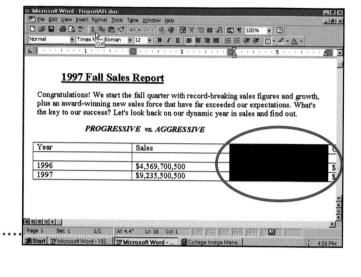

Puzzled?

To delete only the text in a row or column and not the entire row or column, select the text and press the **Delete** key on your keyboard.

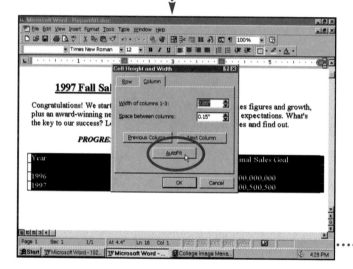

8 If your columns are a little too wide for the amount of text you've entered, you can adjust the space with the Cell Height and Width dialog box. Select the entire table, open the **Table** menu and select **Cell Height and Width**. Click the **Column** tab, then click the **AutoFit** button.

9 Word automatically adjusts the width of the columns to match the length of the cell text in each column. ■

Puzzled?

To return your table column widths back to the default size, open the **Table** menu and select **Distribute Columns Evenly**.

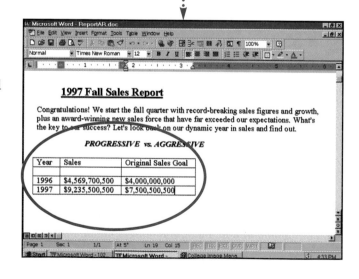

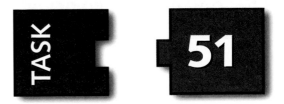

Creating a Two-Column Document

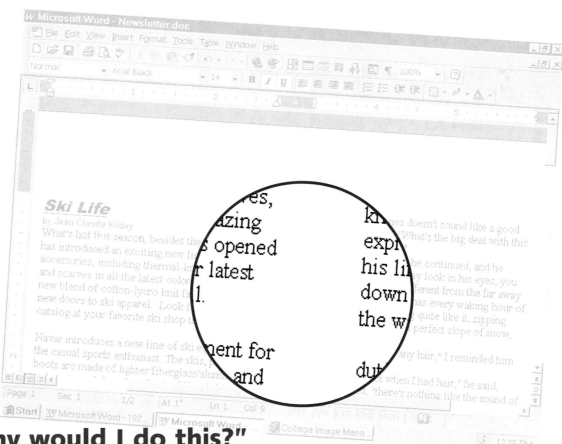

"Why would I do this?"

Are you in charge of the neighborhood newsletter? Need to create a lengthy index for your thesis? Why not use parallel columns? With a two-column document, text flows from one column to the next until all the text is used. Two-column documents work well for newsletters, magazine articles, indexes, and uneven columns for desktop publishing effects.

1 Place the insertion point where you want to create the columns. If you want to turn existing text into columns, select the text. Click the **Page Layout** view button (located to the left of the horizontal scroll bar). You must be in Page Layout view in order to see the columns of text.

Puzzled?

Learn more about Word's view options in Task 54 in Part VIII.

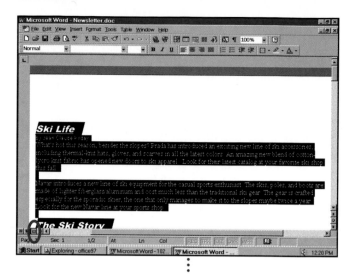

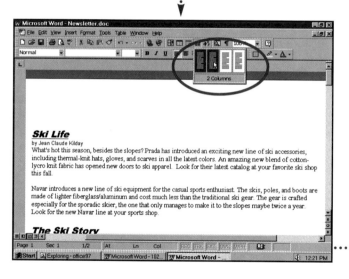

2 Click the **Columns** button (the button with two columns) on the Standard toolbar. A table of column sizes appears. Click the number of columns you want to create.

3 Word creates two columns. You can start entering text to fill the columns. If you used existing text, as shown in the example, you can clearly see the columns in Page Layout view. ■

Puzzled?

To undo the columns, click the **Undo** button on the Standard toolbar immediately. You also can select the text in the columns, click the **Columns** button on the Standard toolbar, and highlight one column.

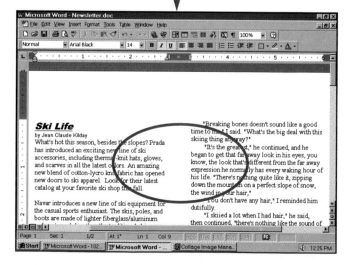

Inserting a WordArt Object

"Why would I do this?"

While you can certainly format text and graphics to add pizzazz to your documents, how about turning text into a piece of art? You can create a special text effect with Microsoft WordArt 2.0. This feature enables you to add designs and shapes to plain text. For example, you can use any TrueType font and arch or tilt the text. WordArt is useful for creating desktop publishing effects.

1 Move the insertion point to where you want to insert the object. Click the **Page Layout** view button (located to the left of the horizontal scroll bar).

Missing Link

You'll need to be in Page Layout view to create a WordArt object. Learn more about Word's view options in Task 54.

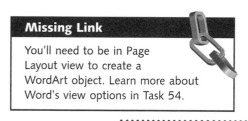

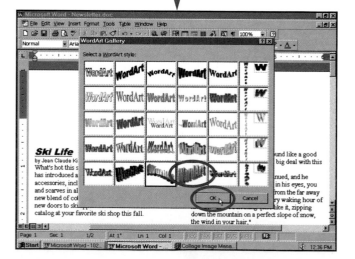

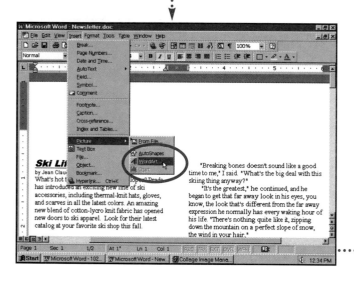

2 Open the **Insert** menu and select **Picture**, then **WordArt**. This opens the WordArt Gallery dialog box.

3 Click the WordArt style you want to use, then click **OK**.

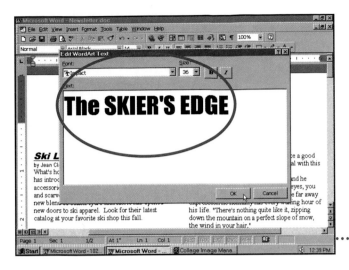

4 The Edit WordArt Text window appears. Type in the text you want to use, replacing the Your Text Here words. Use the **Fonts** drop-down list to specify a new font style. Use the **Size** list to change font sizes. Click **OK** when finished entering your own text.

5 The new WordArt object is added to your document page, along with the WordArt floating toolbar. You'll probably need to make a few adjustments to the size and shape of the object. Drag the selection handles (the tiny boxes that surround the object) to resize and shape the object to fit in the required space.

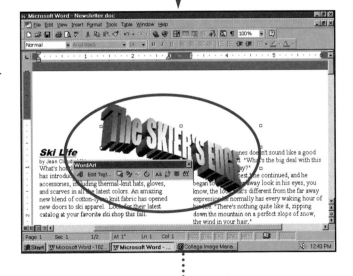

> **Puzzled?**
>
> You may have to make changes to text to make room for the object. You can also move the object around on the document page. Select the object by clicking on it, then drag it to a new location.

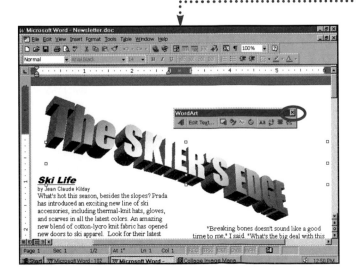

6 Use the WordArt toolbar buttons to modify the WordArt object. For example, you can rotate the object, adjust character spacing, and open a formatting dialog box where you specify word wrapping or color. When finished editing the object, click the **Close** box. (To reopen the toolbar, right-click the object and select **Show WordArt Toolbar**.) ■

> **Missing Link**
>
> To delete the WordArt object, click it once and press **Delete**.

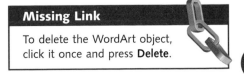

Adding Color to Your Text

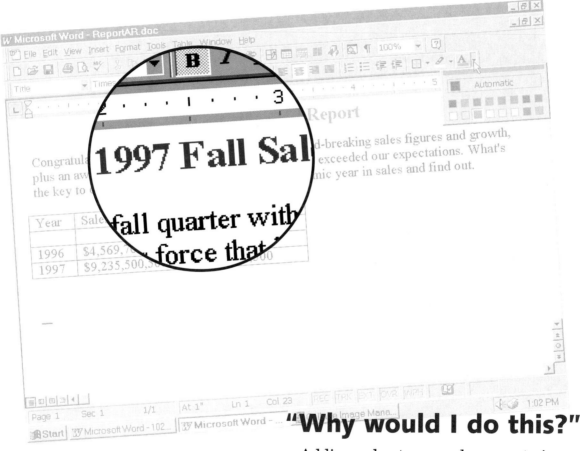

"Why would I do this?"

Adding color to your documents is another way to enhance the presentation of your data. This is particularly true if you're using a color printer. For example, you may want to make the title of your report bright blue to match a folder you've chosen to hold the report. You can easily change the color of your text using Word's Font Color tool, located on the Formatting toolbar.

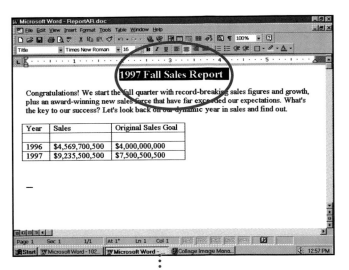

1 Select the text you want to add color to.

Missing Link

With the highlighter pen, you can add a color background behind text. Select the text to highlight, then click the **Highlight** tool on the Formatting toolbar. If you prefer to use another highlighter color, click the down arrow beside the Highlight tool, and select another color from the palette.

2 Click the **Font Color** button on the Formatting toolbar. If you want to choose another color other than the default color, click the down-arrow and select another color from the palette.

Puzzled?

To undo a color, click the **Undo** button on the Standard toolbar immediately after adding a color to your text.

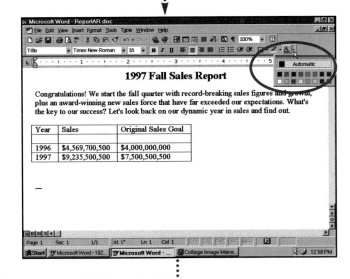

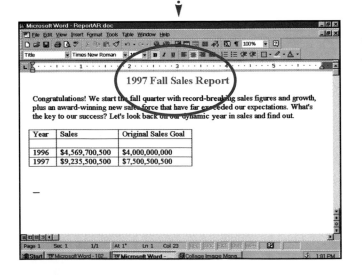

3 Word adds the selected color to your text. When you print the document, the color will print too, assuming you have a color printer. ■

Missing Link

To learn about printing with Word, turn to task 57 in Part VIII. Use your color printer manual for additional help with printing.

PART VIII

Viewing and Printing the Document

ARE YOU READY TO START PRINTING your documents? In this part, you learn how to change the view of your document, preview your document, and then print your document.

Word 97 offers you several ways to view your documents on-screen:

- Normal is the standard editing view. By default, Word starts you in Normal view.

- Page Layout view enables you to display multiple columns, headers and footers, and footnotes as they will be printed.

- Outline view helps you create outlines.

- Online Layout view lets you see what your document would look like as a Web page.

Word's view options let you change your viewing perspective while working with a document. You'll find view buttons for each of these views located in the bottom left corner of your Word screen, to the left of the horizontal scroll bar. To change your view, simply click the appropriate view button. You can also change views using the View menu.

Another feature you'll find helpful when viewing your documents is Word's magnification feature, called Zoom. The Zoom option works with any view. It lets you enlarge or reduce the view of a page on-screen. Text on the screen can be smaller or larger; it may show the whole page or a smaller section of it at higher magnification.

When you're having trouble reading small text, you can easily enlarge the view using the Zoom Control button on the Standard toolbar. You can specify how much of a percentage you want to zoom in or out. You can also open the Zoom dialog box and specify zoom percentages. You'll find the Zoom command on the View menu.

When you're finally ready to print a document, the first thing you should do is use Word's Print Preview feature. Print Preview is a view, but it's not quite like the other views. With Word's Print Preview feature, you can review the appearance of the printed document before you produce the final output. (Unlike the other view options, you can't edit a document in Print Preview.)

When you activate the Print Preview feature, Word opens your document in the Print Preview window, which has it's own tools for viewing the document. The first page of the document appears as a reduced image in the Print Preview window. You can use the Zoom feature in Print Preview to magnify the view. You can also view several pages at once. You can even print the document from the Print Preview window.

Printing is a standard activity these days. In Word, you can print your documents using a basic printing procedure or you can enhance the printout using several page setup options as explained earlier in Part IV. The Print dialog box lets you print some or all of the pages within a document, the current page, a range of pages, selected text, or multiple copies of the printout.

The first time you use your printer with Word, it is a good idea to check the Setup options. Word can use the options and capabilities that are available with each printer. Often, you will need to provide more details about your printer so that Word knows its capabilities. If you want to specify details about your printer, choose the File, Print command and click the Printer button. Then, you can confirm that you installed the right printer and connected it correctly, or you can switch to a different printer.

It is a good idea to save your documents before printing—just in case a printer error or other problem occurs. Therefore, you won't lose the work.

This part introduces you to the basics of viewing and printing your documents. With some experimentation and practice, you will be able to create some very interesting print results.

Displaying a Document in Page Layout View

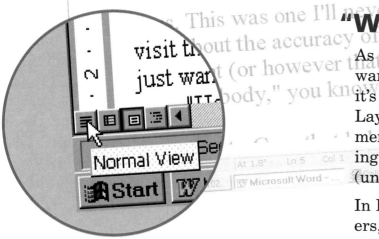

"Why would I do this?"

As you're building a document, you may want to see how it's going to look when it's actually printed out. Word's Page Layout view lets you view your document as it will be printed, while retaining all editing features and capabilities (unlike the Print Preview option).

In Page Layout view, you can see headers, footers, multiple columns, and footnotes in your document. This feature is useful when you are making many formatting changes and need to see the results before committing the text to paper.

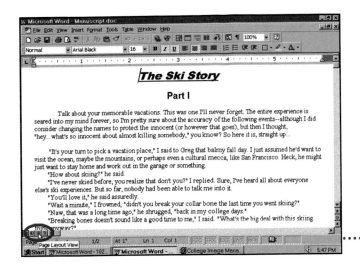

1 Click the **Page Layout View** button (the third view button from the left). This selects the View Page Layout command.

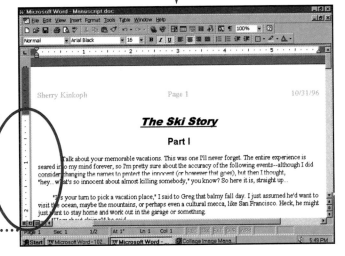

2 Word switches to Page Layout view. In Page Layout view, you can see headers and footers, columns, and other page formatting. A vertical ruler also appears to the left of the document window.

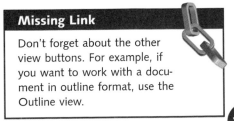

3 To return to Normal view again, click the **Normal View** button (the first view button). This returns the document to normal view. ■

Missing Link

Don't forget about the other view buttons. For example, if you want to work with a document in outline format, use the Outline view.

189

TASK

55

Zooming a Document

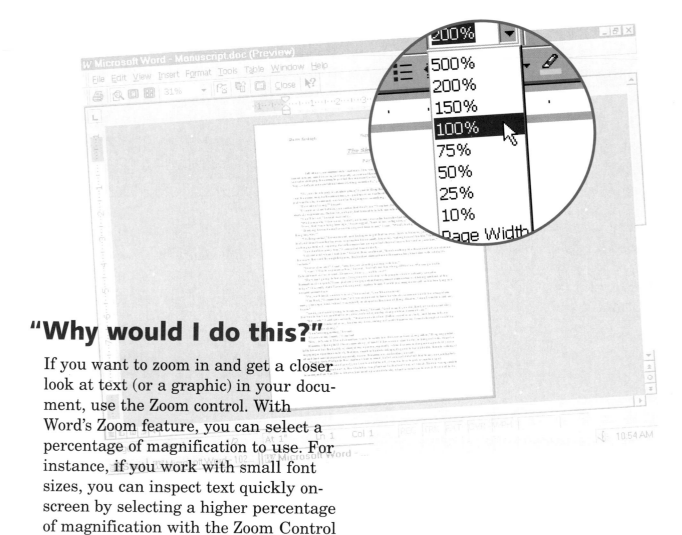

"Why would I do this?"

If you want to zoom in and get a closer look at text (or a graphic) in your document, use the Zoom control. With Word's Zoom feature, you can select a percentage of magnification to use. For instance, if you work with small font sizes, you can inspect text quickly on-screen by selecting a higher percentage of magnification with the Zoom Control button (located on the Standard toolbar). The nice part about zooming in and out of a document is that you don't have to switch view modes or print the file in order to see your work up close.

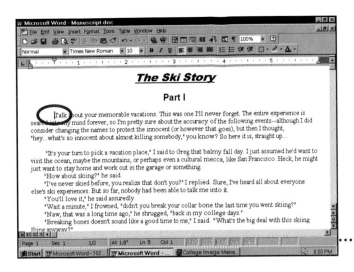

1 Click the insertion point in the area of the screen or text that you want to zoom in on.

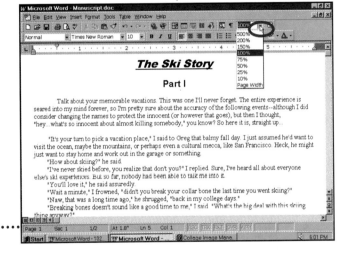

2 Click the **Zoom Control** drop-down arrow to display a list of magnification percentages. (The Zoom Control is located on the Standard toolbar. It's the button showing 100%.)

3 Select a Zoom percentage from the list. For example, if you click **200 percent**, Word will enlarge your document by 200 percent.

191

4 To zoom out your document view, click the **Zoom Control** drop-down arrow again and this time select a lower magnification percentage number. For example, select **50%**.

Puzzled?

If the magnification percentage you want isn't listed in the Zoom Control list, you can type it directly into the Zoom Control text box.

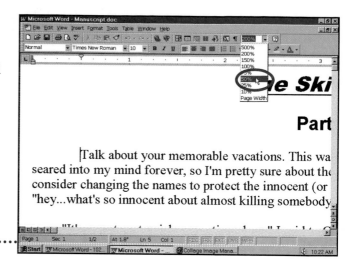

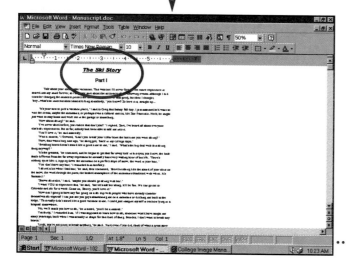

5 Word now reduces the document view to 50 percent.

6 To return to normal magnification, open the Zoom Control list box again and click **100%** to restore the document to 100 percent. ■

Missing Link

To enlarge the document to completely fill the screen horizontally, select **Page Width** from the Zoom Control list box.

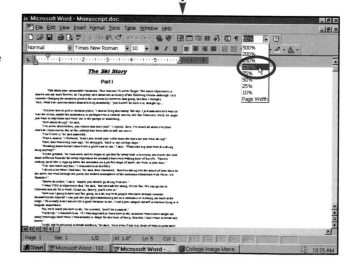

Previewing the Document

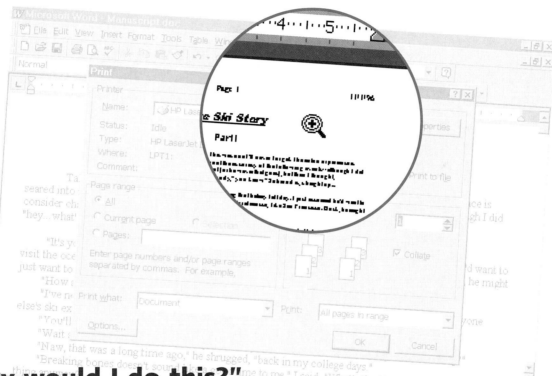

"Why would I do this?"

There's nothing more aggravating than wasting printer paper. You think you've checked over your document only to print it out and find a misplaced heading or paragraph. To make sure things are the way you want them, and to avoid wasting your paper, use Word's Print Preview command to view your document pages before committing them to paper.

The Print Preview command lets you see document pages on-screen as they will appear printed on paper, including page numbers, headers, footers, fonts, fonts sizes and styles, orientation, and margins. Previewing your document is a great way to catch formatting errors, such as incorrect margins, overlapped text, boldfaced text, and other text enhancements. You will save costly printer paper and time by first previewing your document.

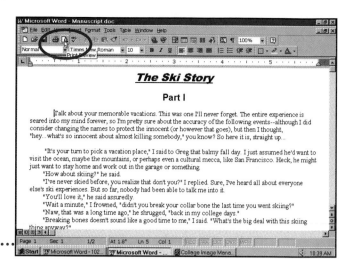

1 Click the **Print Preview** button on the Standard toolbar (the button with the piece of paper and a magnifying glass). Clicking the Print Preview button selects the Print Preview command.

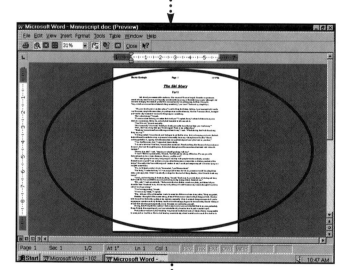

2 The Print Preview window opens and you see a preview of how your document will look when you print it. The Print Preview toolbar has options for viewing the document. (Remember, you can't edit the document from the Print Preview window.)

Puzzled?

Click the **Next Page** button (double down arrow) at the bottom of the scroll bar to see the next page of your document.

3 The mouse pointer (arrow) changes to a magnifying glass and lets you magnify any portion of the page. For example, to get a better look at a particular area on your document page, click the mouse pointer on the area. To zoom back out again, click the mouse pointer again.

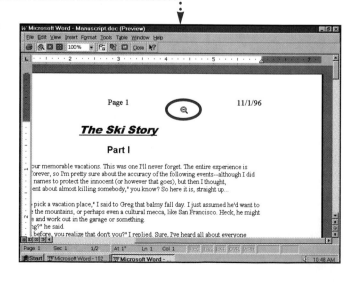

Missing Link

The Zoom Control box on the Print Preview toolbar lets you specify magnification percentages to examine the document up close or far away.

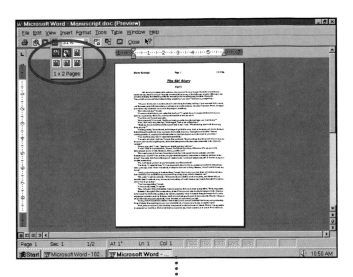

4 To view more than one document page in the Preview window, click the **Multiple Pages** button. A table drops down and you can select the amount of pages you want to view.

Missing Link

You can print from the Print Preview window. Simply click the Print button at the far left end of the Print Preview toolbar.

5 The Print Preview window now shows two document pages. To return to one page on-screen, click the **One Page** button.

Missing Link

Need a ruler? Click the **Ruler** button on the Print Preview toolbar to display both a vertical and horizontal ruler. To turn the ruler off again, click the **Ruler** button again.

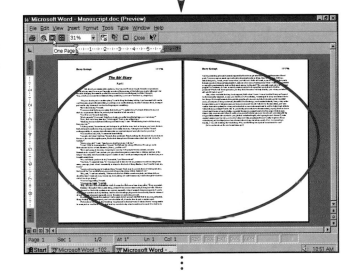

6 To exit Print Preview, click the **Close** button. This returns you to the document. ■

Missing Link

You can also press the **Esc** key to exit the Print Preview window.

TASK 57

Printing the Document

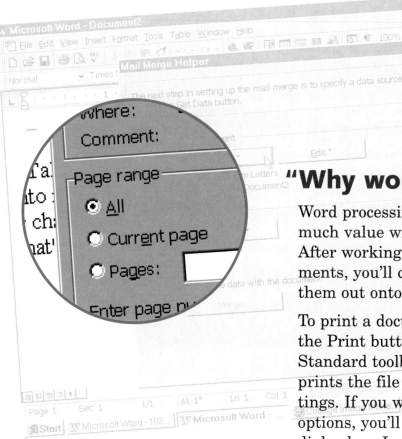

"Why would I do this?"

Word processing programs aren't of much value without printing features. After working hard to create your documents, you'll certainly want to print them out onto paper.

To print a document in Word, just click the Print button located on the Standard toolbar. Word immediately prints the file using any default settings. If you want to change a few options, you'll need to open the Print dialog box. In the Print dialog box, you'll find a variety of print options you can apply to your documents and how they are printed. For example, you can designate the number of copies and collate the copies as you print.

In this task, you'll learn how to use the Print dialog box to produce a hard copy of your document.

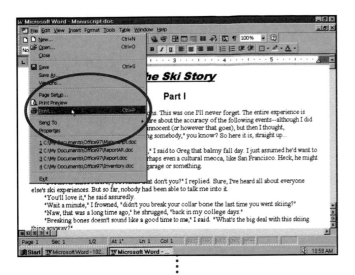

1 Pull down the **File** menu and select **Print**. This opens the Print dialog box. The Print dialog box controls which printer is used, what you print (the entire document, a range of pages, and so on), how many copies you print, and other options.

Missing Link

You can also press **Ctrl+P** on the keyboard to open the Print dialog box.

2 Choose any printing options you want. For example, if you only want Word to print certain pages in the document, click the **Pages** option and specify which pages to print. If you want Word to print more than one copy of the file, use the **Number of copies** box to enter a new number.

Missing Link

To print disconnected pages, enter a comma between the page numbers and page ranges. For example, 1,3,7,9-15,20.

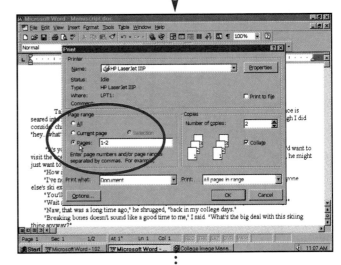

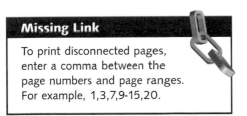

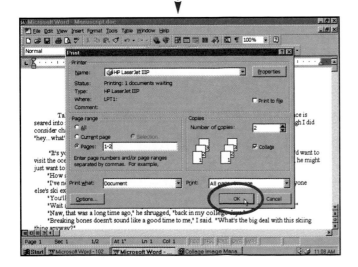

3 Click **OK** to start printing the document. ■

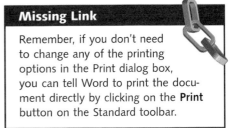

Missing Link

Remember, if you don't need to change any of the printing options in the Print dialog box, you can tell Word to print the document directly by clicking on the **Print** button on the Standard toolbar.

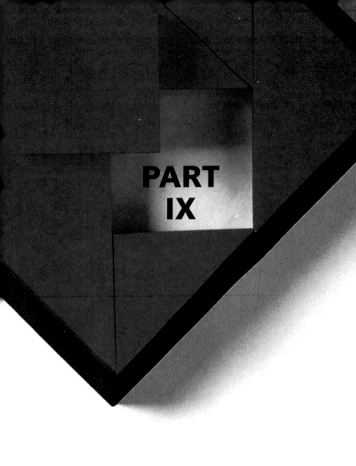

PART
IX

Merging, E-Mailing, and Creating Web Documents

▲ ● ■ ▲ ● ■ ▲ ●

N THIS PART, YOU LEARN HOW TO USE Word 97's communication features to create a form letter using merge tools and to distribute documents in electronic form as e-mail or as a World Wide Web (WWW) document.

Creating form letters is a common task for word processing programs these days. Form letters have many uses in the corporate world (business letters to clients, vendors, and customers) as well as at home (holiday letters, home business correspondence, and more). Two files make up a basic form letter: the data source and the main document. The main document contains the unchanging text and the codes that control the merge. For example, if you're creating a form letter, the main document would contain the body of the letter and fields where the variable data will be inserted. The data source contains the variable information you want inserted into the main document, such as names and addresses. The first several tasks in this part help you create the main document file and the data source file, then to merge the two so that you can print, then mail, your form letters.

Word's Mail Merge feature offers many options that you may want to experiment with on your own. This book provides only the simplest of examples. If you want more information, see your Microsoft Word 97 documentation or Que's *Using Microsoft Word 97*.

This part also shows you how to create envelopes using Word's Mail Merge feature. Word gives you two ways to print addresses on envelopes. If you want to print addresses on envelopes individually, use the Tools, Envelopes and Labels command. Word will print the return address and the mailing address on the envelope or label. However, if you want to print many envelopes at one time, you can use the Merge feature to do a mass mailing. You can also use the Mail Merge feature to print mailing labels.

While you can certainly communicate via the documents you create, there are a few other ways you can use Word 97 to communicate with others. To conclude this part of the book, you'll find some tasks that will help you use Word 97 to send e-mail and create your own Web documents to post on the Internet.

Windows 95 users have the added feature of Microsoft Exchange to help with e-mail (electronic mail) traffic on their computers. Word 97 is designed to work with Microsoft Outlook, Microsoft Exchange, or any other e-mail program you work with. You can mail the documents you create without leaving the Word 97 window. Just open the File menu and select the Send To command. This displays a submenu where you can choose to send the document to someone on your e-mail system, route the document to another user, or fax the document.

Another way to communicate with thousands of people is on the World Wide Web, or Web for short. The Web is just part of the In-ternet, a vast network of many computer networks. The Web it-self is a series of document pages posted on Web servers around the world that use HTML (HyperText Markup Language) codes that include links to other pages. *Links* are simply Web address-es that take you to another Web site when you click them. To access HTML documents, you must typically use a Web browser program, such as Microsoft Internet Explorer.

With Word 97, you can open documents from the Web onto your Word screen and check them out. You also can use Word 97 to help create a Web page yourself to post on the Internet. For tips on what to include on a Web page, use your Web browser (Microsoft Internet Explorer) to surf the Web and view document pages that others have posted.

Word 97 comes with a Web Page Wizard to help you create HTML documents (Web pages). You can insert hyperlinks into your document that jump you to other documents. You'll learn how to create a Web page using Word 97 in this part of the book.

If you're new to the Internet and using the World Wide Web, there are many good books you can read to help you find your way. Check out Que's *Easy Internet*, *Web Publishing with Word for Windows*, and *The Complete Idiot's Guide to the World Wide Web*.

Creating a Main Document

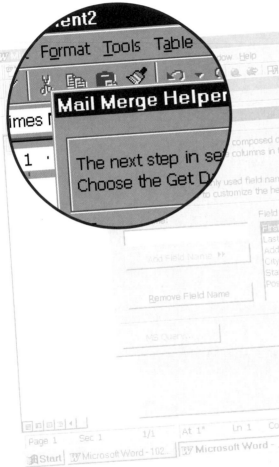

"Why would I do this?"

Instead of typing many individual letters and changing the variable information in each letter, you can tell Word 97 to merge the letter and the variable information, saving you typing and time.

Before you can merge files, you must first open a main document file. The main document file contains field names (for example, {Name} and {Address}) to indicate the information that changes from copy to copy of the merged document. The main document also holds the information that remains constant (for example, the body of the letter and your signature line) in each copy of the merged document. You might want to create a main document that contains an invitation, a product announcement, or a price list. Each field name will be matched up with a field in the data source file. Follow the steps in this task to create a main document file.

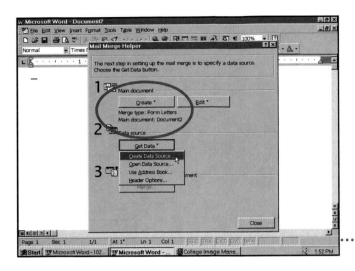

1 Open the **Tools** menu and select **Mail Merge**. Word opens the Merge Mail Helper dialog box.

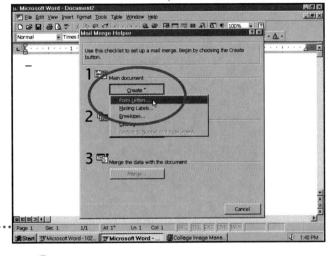

2 Now, select the type of merge file you want to create. Click the **Create** button to display a drop-down list of different merge document formats. To create a form letter, select the **Form Letters** option.

3 Word asks if you want to open a new document or create the document within the current (active) window. Click the **Active Window** button to tell Word that you will use the current window to create the main document. If the window contains an existing document, choose **New Main Document** to open a new file you can use for the main document. You are returned to the Mail Merge Helper dialog box. ■

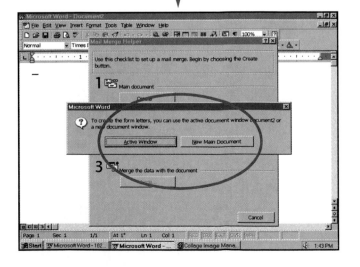

Puzzled?

If you don't want to create the main document, click **Cancel**.

203

Creating and Saving the Data Source

"Why would I do this?"

The data source file stores the variable information that you want to insert into the form fields. Each piece of information is stored in a field, such as, {First Name}; a set of information is called a record (for example, all the information about John Smith). Perhaps you want to create a data source file of addresses for batch mailing. The steps in this task will show you how to select or create fields for the data source file.

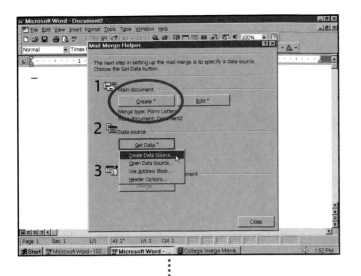

1 From the Mail Merge Helper dialog box, click the **Get Data** button. Word displays a drop-down list of data source options. To create a new data source, select **Create Data Source**. To use an existing database, such as an address book, select **Use Address Book** and designate the appropriate address book to use.

Puzzled?

To use addresses from Microsoft Schedule+, Outlook 97, or Microsoft Exchange, choose **Use Address Book** from the **Get Data** menu.

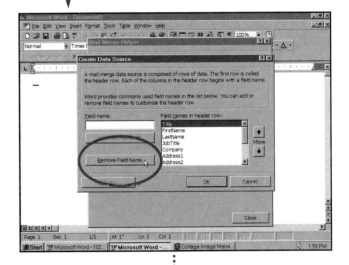

2 If you select Create Data Source, Word opens the Create Data Source dialog box. This box includes a field names list with common field names already entered. Instead of trying to figure out all the fields you'll need, you can eliminate the default fields you don't want. Select a field name from the list that you don't want to use, then click the **Remove Field Name** button.

3 To add a new field name to the list, enter the name in the **Field name** text box and click the **Add Field Name** button. To reorder the fields in the list, use the arrow buttons. Continue deleting, adding, or reordering the field names list until it's complete for your particular form letter.

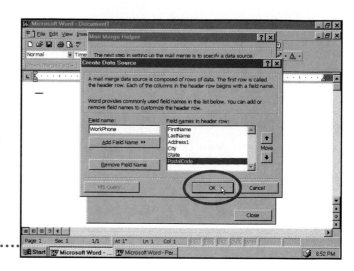

4 When finished creating the field name list, click **OK**.

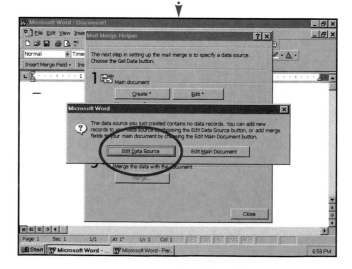

5 The Save As dialog box is displayed so that you can save the field names list as the data source file. Type in a name for the file in the **File Name** text box. Click **Save**.

6 Word prompts you with another dialog box reminding you that no records have been created. Click **Edit Data Source**. This tells Word that you will add the records. The Data Form dialog box appears where you can enter individual records, which you'll learn how to do in the next task. ■

Entering Records into the Data Source

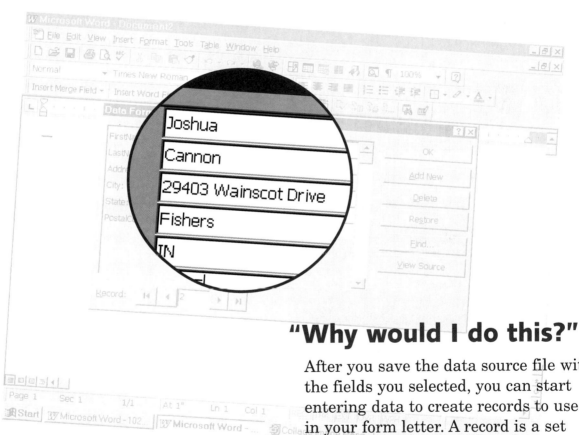

"Why would I do this?"

After you save the data source file with the fields you selected, you can start entering data to create records to use in your form letter. A record is a set of related fields. Each field is a piece of information within a record. For example, {Last Name}, {First Name}, {Address} might be fields in an address database. The record would include the last name, first name, and address for one person.

1 Use the Data Form dialog box to enter as many records as you need. Fill in each field with the appropriate text; use the **Tab** key to move from field to field (use **Shift+Tab** to move back to a previous field). You can also press **Enter** to move to the next field.

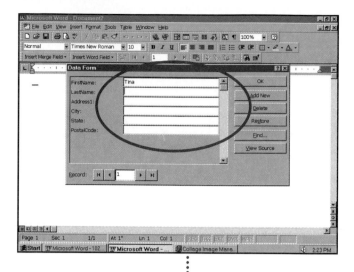

Puzzled?

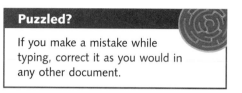

If you make a mistake while typing, correct it as you would in any other document.

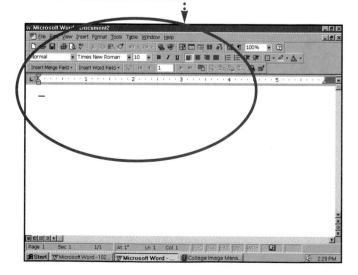

2 When you're ready to enter the next record, click the **Add New** button or press **Enter** from the last entry. The Data Form's text boxes clear and you can enter another record. Continue adding new records as needed.

Missing Link

The Record box at the bottom of the Data Form box tells you how many records you've entered. You can use the arrow buttons to revisit any of the records you type in or move backward and forward in the record's list.

3 When finished creating the records you need to use with the form letter, click **OK**. This returns you to the main document where you'll see the Mail Merge toolbar displayed. In the next task, you will type the main document's body text. ■

Missing Link

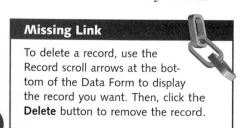

To delete a record, use the Record scroll arrows at the bottom of the Data Form to display the record you want. Then, click the **Delete** button to remove the record.

Typing the Main Document

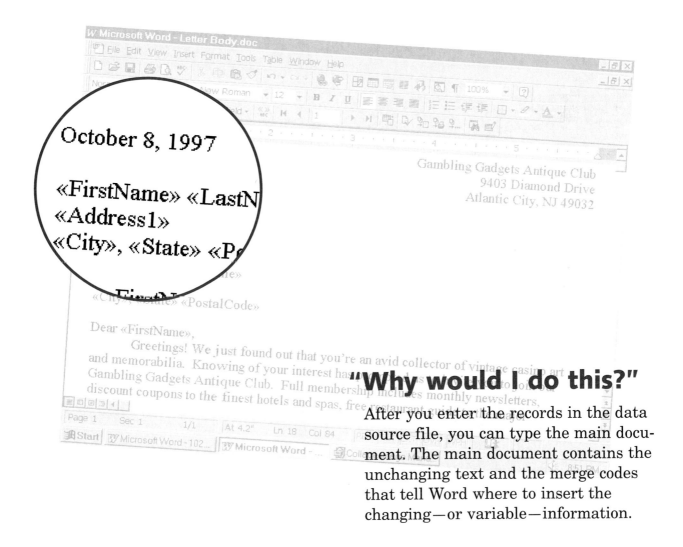

W Microsoft Word - Letter Body.doc

File Edit View Insert Format Tools Table Window Help

New Roman   12   B   I   U

October 8, 1997

«FirstName» «LastN
«Address1»
«City», «State» «P

Gambling Gadgets Antique Club
9403 Diamond Drive
Atlantic City, NJ 49032

«City», «State» «PostalCode»

Dear «FirstName»,

Greetings! We just found out that you're an avid collector of vintage casino art and memorabilia. Knowing of your interest has... Gambling Gadgets Antique Club. Full membership includes monthly newsletters, discount coupons to the finest hotels and spas, free restaurant...

Page 1   Sec 1   1/1   At 4.2"   Ln 18   Col 84

Start   Microsoft Word - 102...   Microsoft Word -

"Why would I do this?"

After you enter the records in the data source file, you can type the main document. The main document contains the unchanging text and the merge codes that tell Word where to insert the changing—or variable—information.

1 Type in the body text for your form letter. When you reach an area in your document where you want to insert a field (variable information), click the **Insert Merge Field** button on the Mail Merge toolbar. This displays a drop-down list of field names you created in Task 59. Select the field name you want to insert.

Puzzled?

If you make a mistake while typing, correct it as you would in any regular document.

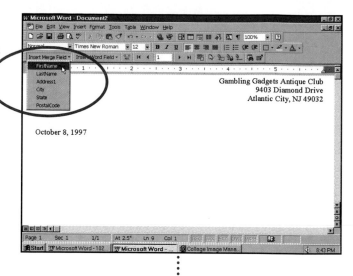

2 The field is inserted into the document and set apart with brackets, as shown in the figure. Continue building your form letter, inserting fields as needed. You can separate fields with spaces or punctuation as necessary.

Missing Link

If you insert the field incorrectly, select it and press the **Delete** key. Then, try again.

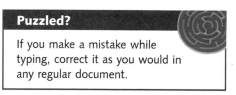

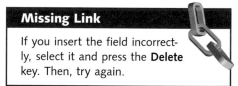

3 To save the main document with the field codes, click the **Save** button on the Standard toolbar. This opens the Save As dialog box. Type in a name for the file in the **File Name** text box. Click the **Save** button to save the document. This completes the letter. To merge the letter with the records you created in Task 60, see the next task. ■

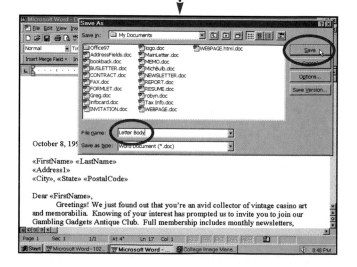

Merging the Files

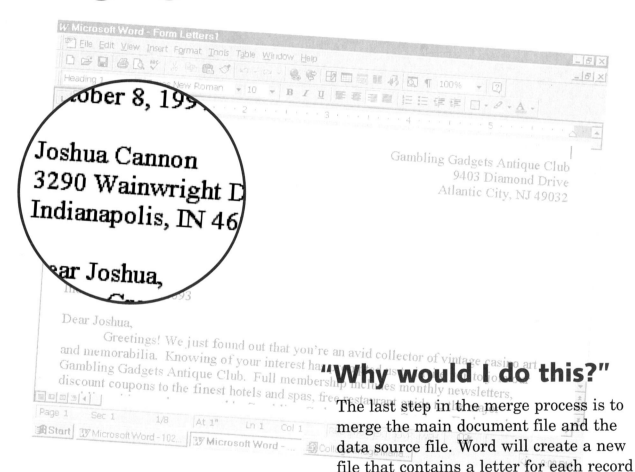

"Why would I do this?"

The last step in the merge process is to merge the main document file and the data source file. Word will create a new file that contains a letter for each record in the data source. You can save the new file or just print it. The Mail Merge feature offers many options that enable you to control how a merge is performed. For example, you can merge to the printer or merge all letters into a document with one letter displayed per page.

1 Click the **Mail Merge Helper** button on the Mail Merge toolbar (seventh button from the right end of the toolbar). The Mail Merge Helper dialog box appears. Click the **Merge** button.

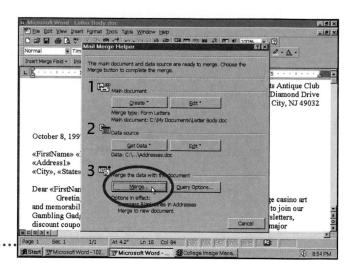

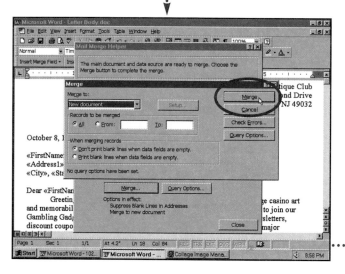

2 The Merge dialog box appears. Options here enable you to control which records are merged, where the letters are created, and other choices. Here the default options are acceptable. Click the **Merge** button.

3 Word creates a custom letter for each record in the data source file. The form letter's text is the same. For each field code, information is pulled from the data source and inserted into the form letter. You can now save the file using a new name, or print it out using your printer. ■

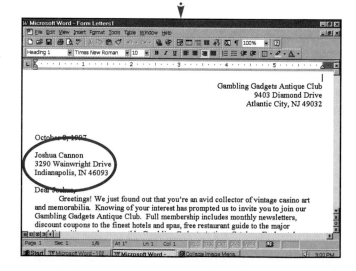

Puzzled?

If the merge didn't go as planned, check to make sure you set up each file correctly.

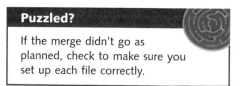

Creating Envelopes

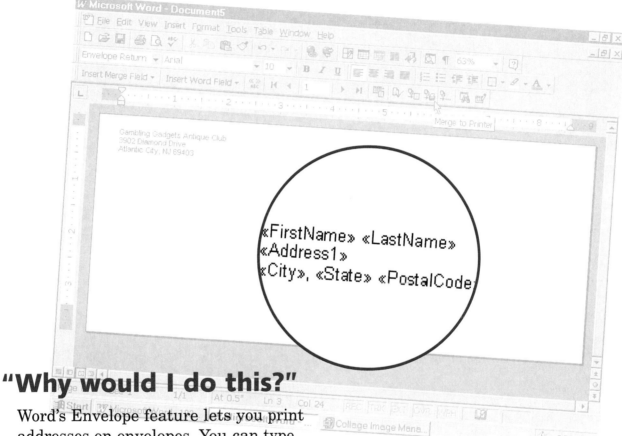

"Why would I do this?"

Word's Envelope feature lets you print addresses on envelopes. You can type the return address and then use the Mail Merge feature to print the mailing addresses on the envelopes. You can also use the Mail Merge feature to create labels, too. In order to use Mail Merge to make envelopes, you must have a printer that can print on envelopes.

Task 63: Creating Envelopes

1 Open the **Tools** menu and choose **Mail Merge** to display the Tools Mail Merge Helper dialog box. Click the **Create** button and select **Envelopes**. This tells Word that you are creating envelopes.

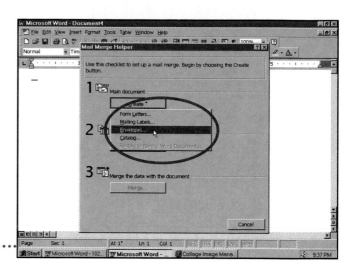

2 You are prompted whether you want to change the document type or create a new main document. Click **New Main Document**. You are returned to the Mail Merge Helper dialog box. Next, select a data source for merging.

3 From the Mail Merge Helper dialog box, click the **Get Data** button and select **Open Data Source**. This displays the Open Data Source dialog box.

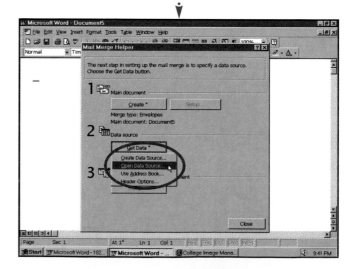

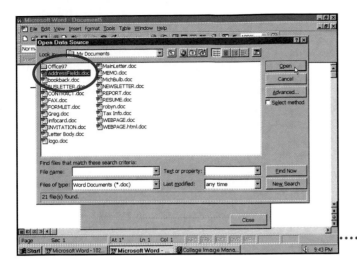

4 Double-click the data source file you want to use. This tells Word to open the data file containing your address records.

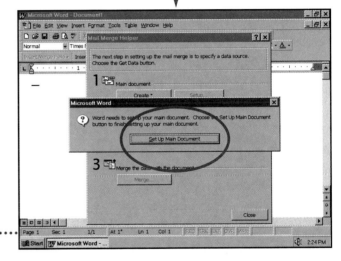

5 Word prompts you to set up the main document for the envelopes. Click the **Set Up Main Document** button.

6 You see the Envelope Options dialog box. Here the default options are acceptable. Click **OK** to continue.

215

7 The Envelope Address dialog box appears. Use this box to designate which fields are to be used on the envelopes. Click the **Insert Merge Field** button and choose a field. The fields listed are the default merge fields for merging envelopes. Repeat this step for each merge field you want to include, as shown in the sample fields in the figure. When finished, click **OK**, then click **Close**.

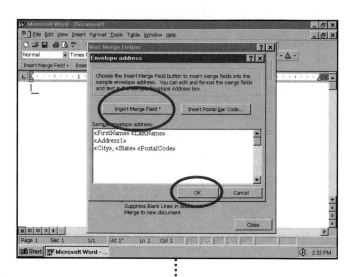

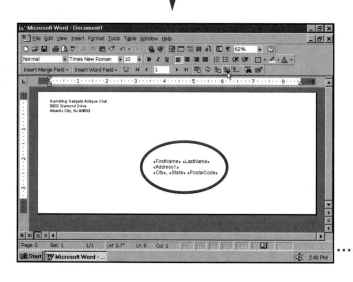

8 Type or edit the return address on the envelope form. Save the file and give it a name, such as ENVELOPE. Click the **Merge to Printer** button on the Mail Merge toolbar (fourth button from the right side).

9 The Print dialog box opens. Insert an envelope in the printer or use an envelope tray to feed envelopes into your printer. Then click **OK** to start printing addresses on the envelopes. ■

Puzzled?

If the merge didn't go as planned, check that you set up each file correctly.

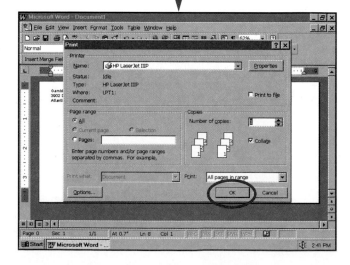

E-Mailing a Document

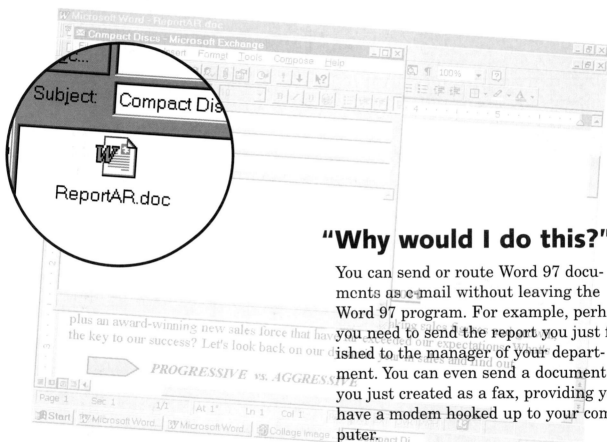

"Why would I do this?"

You can send or route Word 97 documents as e-mail without leaving the Word 97 program. For example, perhaps you need to send the report you just finished to the manager of your department. You can even send a document you just created as a fax, providing you have a modem hooked up to your computer.

Word makes it easy to send the documents you create to other people. To do so, Word works with the e-mail system that's in use for your computer, such as Microsoft Outlook, Microsoft Exchange, or another mail program. You must have an e-mail program like one of these installed on your computer system for the steps in this task to work.

Task 64: E-Mailing a Document

1 Open the document you want to e-mail onto the Word 97 screen. Pull down the **File** menu and select **Send To**. A sub-menu appears. To e-mail the document, select **Mail Recipient**.

Missing Link

You can also route documents or send them as faxes. Select the appropriate command from the Send To menu and designate how you want the document handled using Microsoft Outlook or Exchange.

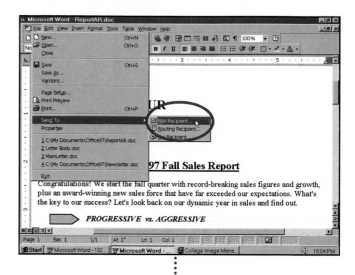

2 An e-mail window opens on your screen. Notice the Word document appears as part of the e-mail message, as an attached file. Click the **To** button and select a recipient to mail the document to from your address book. To give the message a title, type one in the **Subject** text box.

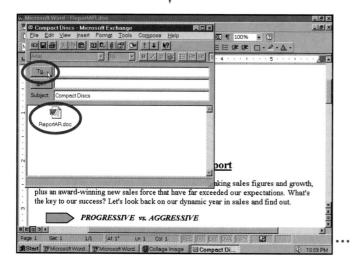

3 When you're ready to send the file, click the **Send** button, the first button on the Exchange toolbar. This sends the file to the Outbox for your e-mail program. Then, you need to open your e-mail program, open your Outbox, select the message with the Word document, then use your e-mail program's Send command to send the message. ■

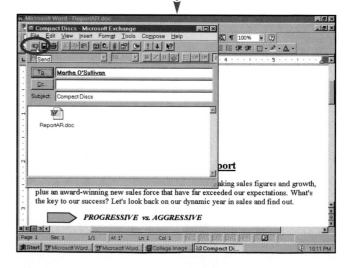

Creating a Web Document Using Templates

"Why would I do this?"

Ready to make your own Web page? It seems like everybody is getting into the World Wide Web these days, and posting their own Web pages for others to view. Word 97 comes with templates you can use to help create a Web page document. If your Internet service provider allows, you can save a Word document as an HTML file and post it on the provider's Web server for others to access. Be sure to check with your service provider first to find out how to publish the page after you've created it.

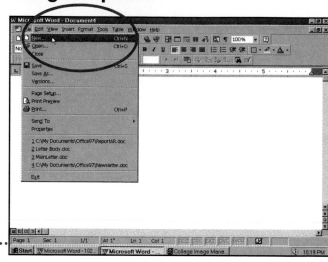

1 Open the **File** menu and select **New**. (You must use the File menu to access Word's templates. You won't be able to using the New button on the Standard toolbar.)

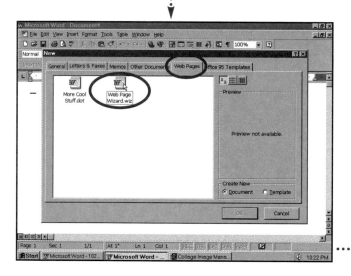

2 Word opens the New dialog box. Click the **Web Pages** tab. To use the Web Page Wizard to help you create a Web page, double-click the **Web Page Wizard.wiz** icon.

3 Word opens a sample Web page document you can use to build your own page. Read the instructions on the template for replacing the sample text with your own text.

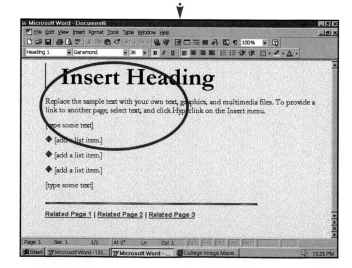

Missing Link

You can add graphics to your Web pages using Word's Insert Picture command, or you can draw your own shapes with Word's drawing tools. Check Tasks 46 and 47 for more information.

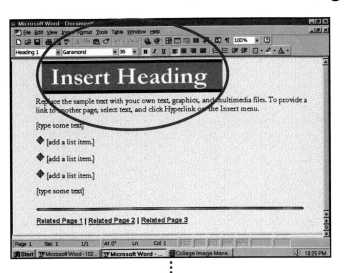

4 To start adding your own text to the page, click the area you want to change. This selects the template text, as shown in the figure. Type in your own text to replace the template's sample text. Continue replacing the existing text with your own text and building the page.

Missing Link

You can use Word's formatting commands to change the look of your text. For example, you can make the text bold, larger, or change font styles.

5 When you find a place on the page where you want to insert a link to another Web page, open the **Insert** menu and select **Hyperlink**. This opens the Insert Hyperlink dialog box. Type in the link (or URL) you want to use in the **Link to file or URL** text box. If you're not sure about the link's location, click the **Browse** button to locate it.

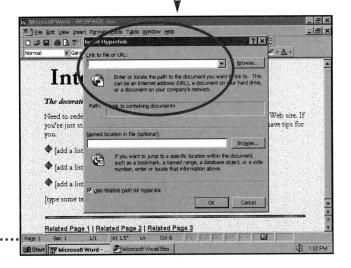

6 When finished, click the **OK** button and the link is added to your page. When the page is finished, save the file as an HTML document by adding the extension **.htm** to the file name in the Save As dialog box. ■

Missing Link

To post your new Web document onto a Web server, check with your Internet service provider to find out if they'll let you have access rights and that their server will support saving files.

PART X

Sample Documents

- ◆ Create a Memo

- ◆ Create a Business Letter

- ◆ Create a Report

- ◆ Create a Resume

- ◆ Create a Newsletter

- ◆ Create an Invitation

- ◆ Create a Contract

- ◆ Create a Fax Cover Sheet

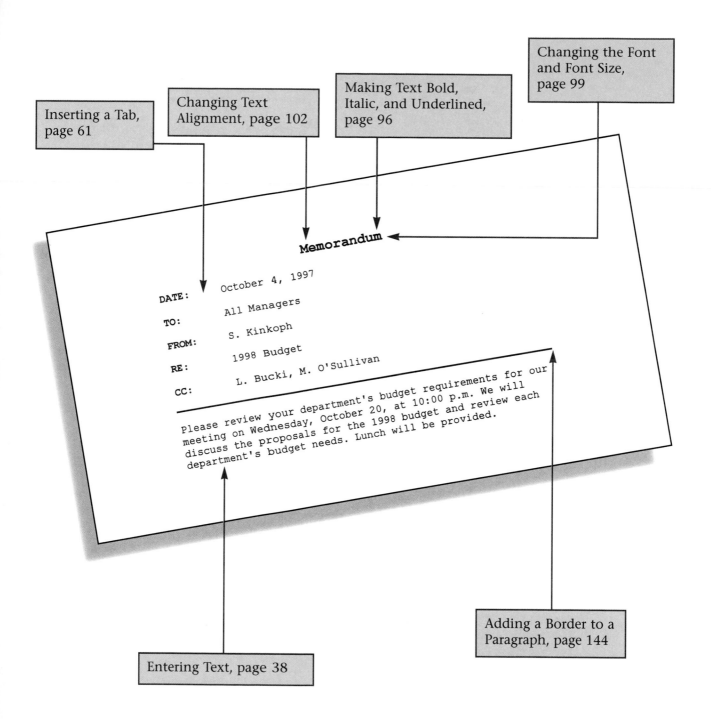

Inserting a Tab, page 61

Changing Text Alignment, page 102

Making Text Bold, Italic, and Underlined, page 96

Changing the Font and Font Size, page 99

Memorandum

DATE: October 4, 1997

TO: All Managers

FROM: S. Kinkoph

RE: 1998 Budget

CC: L. Bucki, M. O'Sullivan

Please review your department's budget requirements for our meeting on Wednesday, October 20, at 10:00 p.m. We will discuss the proposals for the 1998 budget and review each department's budget needs. Lunch will be provided.

Adding a Border to a Paragraph, page 144

Entering Text, page 38

Create a Memo

1 The heading is centered at the top of the memo. The font is Courier New, 16 point, boldface. Use these tasks to help create the same look:

Changing Text Alignment	*TASK 29, p. 102*
Changing the Font and Font Size	*TASK 28, p. 99*
Making Text Bold, Italic, and Underlined	*TASK 27, p. 96*

2 The remaining memo text is Courier New, 12 point. To create the memo address as shown in the sample, type **DATE:**, press **Tab**, and insert the date. Type **TO:**, press **Tab**, and type the name or names of the memo recipients. Do this for each line of the memo address. See these tasks for assistance:

Changing the Font and Font Size	*TASK 28, p. 99*
Inserting a Tab	*TASK 17, p. 61*
Inserting the Date	*TASK 39, p. 135*

3 Press **Enter** and add a few blank lines between the memo address and the memo contents. Type in the memo contents. See this task:

Entering Text	*TASK 9, p. 38*

4 Add a line between the memo address and the memo contents. The line in the sample is a double 1/2-point line style. See this task for help:

Adding a Border to a Paragraph	*TASK 41, p. 144*

5 Save and print the memo. See these tasks on saving and printing:

Saving a Document	*TASK 20, p. 72*
Printing the Document	*TASK 57, p. 196*

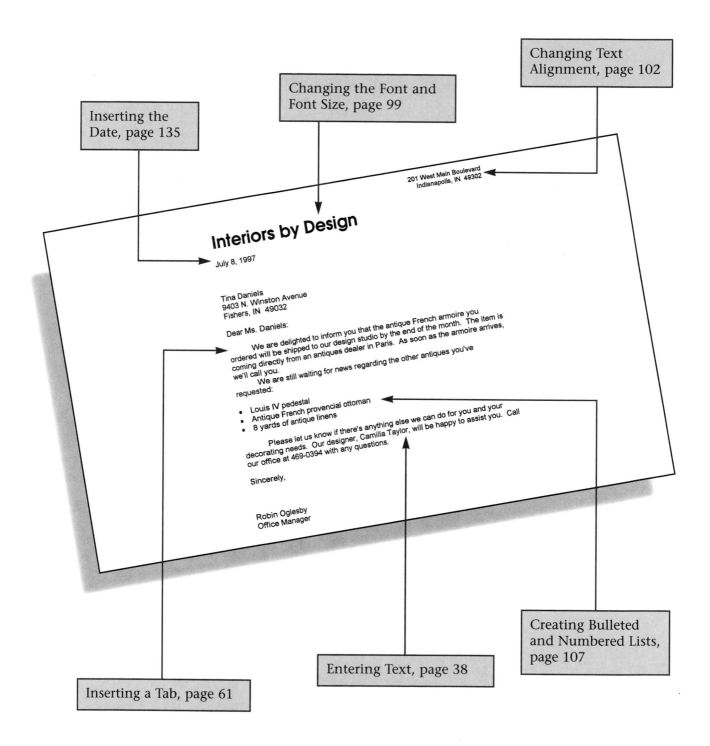

Changing Text Alignment, page 102

Changing the Font and Font Size, page 99

Inserting the Date, page 135

201 West Main Boulevard
Indianapolis, IN 49302

Interiors by Design

July 8, 1997

Tina Daniels
9403 N. Winston Avenue
Fishers, IN 49032

Dear Ms. Daniels:

We are delighted to inform you that the antique French armoire you ordered will be shipped to our design studio by the end of the month. The item is coming directly from an antiques dealer in Paris. As soon as the armoire arrives, we'll call you.

We are still waiting for news regarding the other antiques you've requested:

- Louis IV pedestal
- Antique French provencial ottoman
- 8 yards of antique linens

Please let us know if there's anything else we can do for you and your decorating needs. Our designer, Camilla Taylor, will be happy to assist you. Call our office at 469-0394 with any questions.

Sincerely,

Robin Oglesby
Office Manager

Creating Bulleted and Numbered Lists, page 107

Entering Text, page 38

Inserting a Tab, page 61

Create a Business Letter

1 The return address is right-aligned at the top of the document. The font used is Arial, 10 point type. See these tasks for assistance in creating the same look:

Changing the Font and Font Size	*TASK 28, p. 99*
Entering Text	*TASK 9, p. 38*
Changing Text Alignment	*TASK 29, p. 102*

2 The company name really stands out, using the font Avalon, 26 point, and boldface. See these tasks:

Changing the Font and Font Size	*TASK 28, p. 99*
Making Text Bold, Italic, and Underlined	*TASK 27, p. 96*

3 Below the company name is the date. Use Word's automatic date feature to insert the date. This task explains how to complete this step:

Inserting the Date	*TASK 39, p. 135*

4 The body of the letter uses Arial, 12 point. Use the Tab key to indent the paragraphs. Use the Enter key to add extra space between lines and paragraphs, as needed. Use the Bulleted List toolbar button to create bulleted lists you might need. See these tasks for help:

Changing the Font and Font Size	*TASK 28, p. 99*
Entering Text	*TASK 9, p. 38*
Inserting a Tab	*TASK 17, p. 61*
Creating Bulleted and Numbered Lists	*TASK 31, p. 107*

5 Save and print the letter. See these tasks on saving and printing:

Saving a Document	*TASK 20, p. 72*
Printing the Document	*TASK 57, p. 196*

Shading a Paragraph, page 148

Changing the Font and Font Size, page 99

Making Text Bold, Italic, and Underlined, page 96

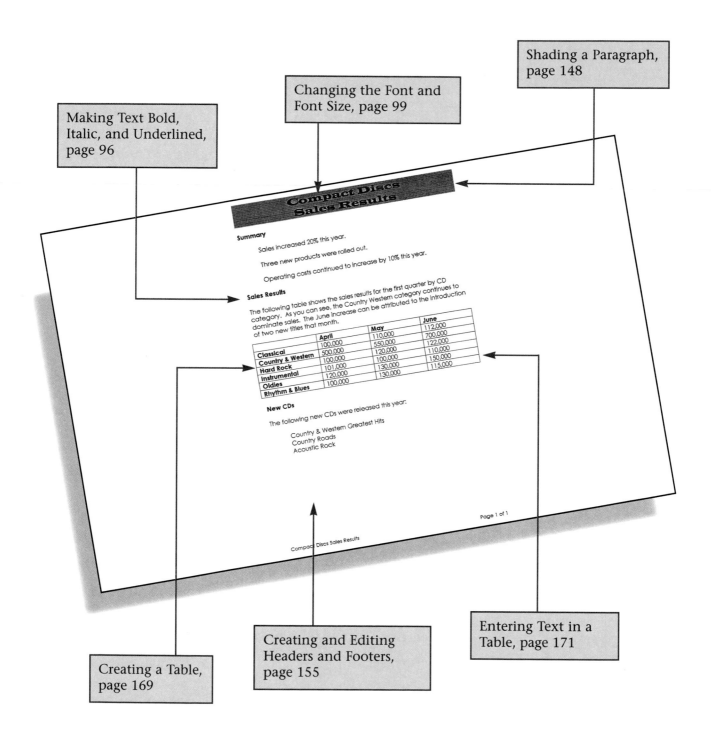

Entering Text in a Table, page 171

Creating and Editing Headers and Footers, page 155

Creating a Table, page 169

Create a Report

1 The report name is centered and created with the font Wide Latin, 18 point. A paragraph border and a paragraph shade are added to make the name pop out. These tasks cover how to apply the formatting changes:

Changing Text Alignment   *TASK 29, p. 102*

Making Text Bold, Italic, and Underlined   *TASK 27, p. 96*

Changing the Font and Font Size   *TASK 28, p. 99*

Shading a Paragraph   *TASK 42, p. 148*

2 The report's body text is in Century Gothic, 12-point type. The headings are bold. A table has been added to enhance a tabbed list of statistics. Here are the tasks to help with this step:

Entering Text   *TASK 9, p. 38*

Changing the Font and Font Size   *TASK 28, p. 99*

Making Text Bold, Italic, and Underlined   *TASK 27, p. 96*

Creating a Table   *TASK 47, p. 166*

Entering Text in a Table   *TASK 48, p. 169*

3 A footer with the report name and page number is added to the bottom of the report. The page number is right-aligned. See these tasks:

Creating and Editing Headers and Footers   *TASK 45, p. 155*

Changing Text Alignment   *TASK 29, p. 102*

4 Save and print the report. See these tasks on saving and printing:

Saving a Document   *TASK 20, p. 72*

Printing the Document   *TASK 57, p. 196*

Changing the Font and Font Size, page 99

Changing Text Alignment, page 102

Adding a Border to a Paragraph, page 144

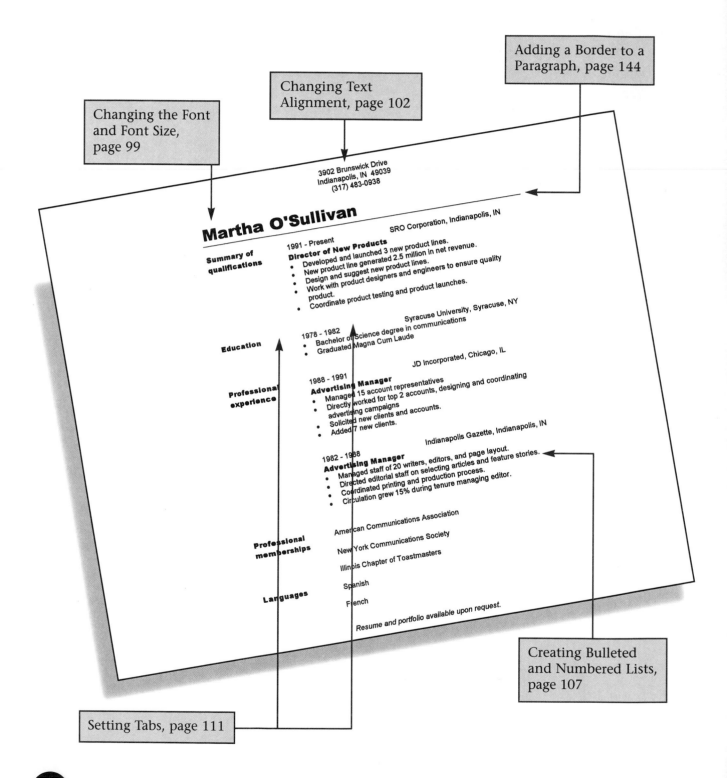

3902 Brunswick Drive
Indianapolis, IN 49039
(317) 483-0938

Martha O'Sullivan

Summary of qualifications

SRO Corporation, Indianapolis, IN

1991 - Present
Director of New Products
- Developed and launched 3 new product lines.
- New product line generated 2.5 million in net revenue.
- Design and suggest new product lines.
- Work with product designers and engineers to ensure quality product.
- Coordinate product testing and product launches.

Education

Syracuse University, Syracuse, NY

1978 - 1982
- Bachelor of Science degree in communications
- Graduated Magna Cum Laude

Professional experience

JD Incorporated, Chicago, IL

1988 - 1991
Advertising Manager
- Managed 15 account representatives
- Directly worked for top 2 accounts, designing and coordinating advertising campaigns
- Solicited new clients and accounts.
- Added 7 new clients.

Indianapolis Gazette, Indianapolis, IN

1982 - 1988
Advertising Manager
- Managed staff of 20 writers, editors, and page layout.
- Directed editorial staff on selecting articles and feature stories.
- Coordinated printing and production process.
- Circulation grew 15% during tenure managing editor.

Professional memberships

American Communications Association

New York Communications Society

Illinois Chapter of Toastmasters

Languages

Spanish

French

Resume and portfolio available upon request.

Creating Bulleted and Numbered Lists, page 107

Setting Tabs, page 111

Create a Resume

1 The address and phone number are centered across the top of the document. The font used is Arial, 10 point type. See these tasks:

Changing the Font and Font Size   *TASK 28, p. 99*

Entering Text   *TASK 9, p. 38*

Changing Text Alignment   *TASK 29, p. 102*

2 The name, in this example, uses Arial Black, 22 point type. A horizontal line is added underneath the name. See these tasks:

Changing the Font and Font Size   *TASK 28, p. 99*

Adding a Border to a Paragraph   *TASK 41, p. 144*

3 The body of the resume is set in Arial, 10 point type, headings in Arial Black. Bulleted lists and tabs are used to layout the text in an attractive, easy-to-read format. Use these tasks:

Entering Text   *TASK 9, p. 38*

Setting Tabs   *TASK 32, p. 111*

Changing the Font and Font Size   *TASK 28, p. 99*

Creating Bulleted and Numbered Lists   *TASK 31, p. 107*

4 Save and print the resume. See these tasks on saving and printing:

Saving a Document   *TASK 20, p. 72*

Printing the Document   *TASK 57, p. 196*

Changing the Font and Font Size, page 99

Adding a Border to a Paragraph, page 144

Setting Tabs, page 111

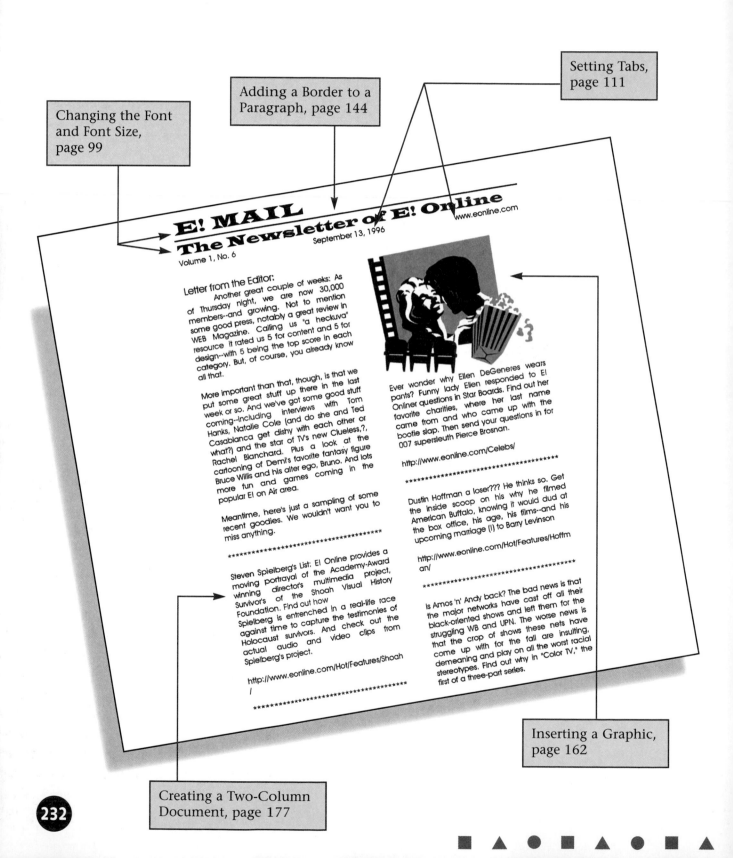

E! MAIL
The Newsletter of E! Online
www.eonline.com
September 13, 1996
Volume 1, No. 6

Letter from the Editor:
Another great couple of weeks: As of Thursday night, we are now 30,000 members--and growing. Not to mention some good press, notably a great review in WEB Magazine. Calling us "a heckuva" resource it rated us 5 for content and 5 for design--with 5 being the top score in each category. But, of course, you already know all that.

More important than that, though, is that we put some great stuff up there in the last week or so. And we've got some good stuff coming--including interviews with Tom Hanks, Natalie Cole (and do she and Ted Casablanca get dishy with each other or what?) and the star of TV's new Clueless,?, Rachel Blanchard. Plus a look at the cartooning of Demi's favorite fantasy figure Bruce Willis and his alter ego, Bruno. And lots more fun and games coming in the popular E! on Air area.

Meantime, here's just a sampling of some recent goodies. We wouldn't want you to miss anything.

****

Steven Spielberg's List: E! Online provides a moving portrayal of the Academy-Award winning director's multimedia project, Survivor's of the Shoah Visual History Foundation. Find out how Spielberg is entrenched in a real-life race against time to capture the testimonies of Holocaust survivors. And check out the actual audio and video clips from Spielberg's project.

http://www.eonline.com/Hot/Features/Shoah/

****

Ever wonder why Ellen DeGeneres wears pants? Funny lady Ellen responded to E! Onliner questions in Star Boards. Find out her favorite charities, where her last name came from and who came up with the bootie slap. Then send your questions in for 007 supersleuth Pierce Brosnan.

http://www.eonline.com/Celebs/

****

Dustin Hoffman a loser??? He thinks so. Get the inside scoop on his why he filmed American Buffalo, knowing it would dud at the box office, his age, his films--and his upcoming marriage (!) to Barry Levinson

http://www.eonline.com/Hot/Features/Hoffman/

****

Is Amos 'n' Andy back? The bad news is that the major networks have cast off all their black-oriented shows and left them for the struggling WB and UPN. The worse news is that the crop of shows these nets have come up with for the fall are insulting, demeaning and play on all the worst racial stereotypes. Find out why in "Color TV," the first of a three-part series.

Inserting a Graphic, page 162

Creating a Two-Column Document, page 177

Create a Newsletter

1 The newsletter banner consists of three lines of text. The top line is set in Wide Latin, 22 point type. The second line is set in Wide Latin, 18 point type. The Third line is set in Avante Garde BK BT, 10 point and tabs are used to space the text. See these tasks for help:

Making Text Bold, Italic, and Underlined	*TASK 27, p. 96*
Changing the Font and Font Size	*TASK 28, p. 99*
Setting Tabs	*TASK 32, p. 111*

2 A line has been added below the first banner text using the Borders and Shading commands. See this task:

Adding a Border to a Paragraph	*TASK 41, p. 144*

3 The newsletter's body text is set in Avante Garde BK BT, 10 point type, headings in Avante Garde BK BT, 14 point type and boldface. See these tasks:

Making Text Bold, Italic, and Underlined	*TASK 27, p. 96*
Changing the Font and Font Size	*TASK 28, p. 99*

4 The body text is formatted into a two-column format using Word's Column command. See the task below for help:

Creating a Two-Column Document	*TASK 51, p. 177*

5 A graphic has been added to illustrate the newsletter and resized to fit. See the following task:

Inserting a Graphic	*TASK 46, p. 162*

6 Save and print the newsletter. See these tasks on saving and printing:

Saving a Document	*TASK 20, p. 72*
Printing the Document	*TASK 57, p. 196*

Changing the Font and
Font Size, page 99

Join us for a tea party!

When:
Saturday, April 19th
3:00 p.m.

Where:
The Pavillion at 10th Street
Englebert, New York

R.S.V.P.:
Victoria Chancellor
849-0594

Inserting a Graphic,
page 162

Create an Invitation

1 To create a half-page invitation, open the **File** menu and select **Page Setup** and customize the paper size by clicking on the Paper Size tab in the Page Setup dialog box. Set the height to 5 inches instead of 11. Click the **Margins** tab and reset any margin settings as needed. Use this task:

Changing Margins	*TASK 33, p. 114*

2 To set a border around the page, open the Borders and Shading dialog box, click the **Page Border** tab and select a border style to use. See this task for help:

Adding a Border to a Paragraph	*TASK 41, p. 144*

3 Insert a graphic and adjust the text wrap. See this task for help:

Inserting a Graphic	*TASK 46, p. 162*

4 The first line of invitation text is set in Shelley Volante BT, 28 point type. The remaining invitation text is set in Gatineau, 14 point type, and the headings are boldface. See these tasks:

Entering Text	*TASK 9, p. 38*
Changing the Font and Font Size	*TASK 28, p. 99*
Making Text Bold, Italic, and Underlined	*TASK 27, p. 96*

5 Save and print the invitation. See these tasks on saving and printing:

Saving a Document	*TASK 20, p. 72*
Printing the Document	*TASK 57, p. 196*

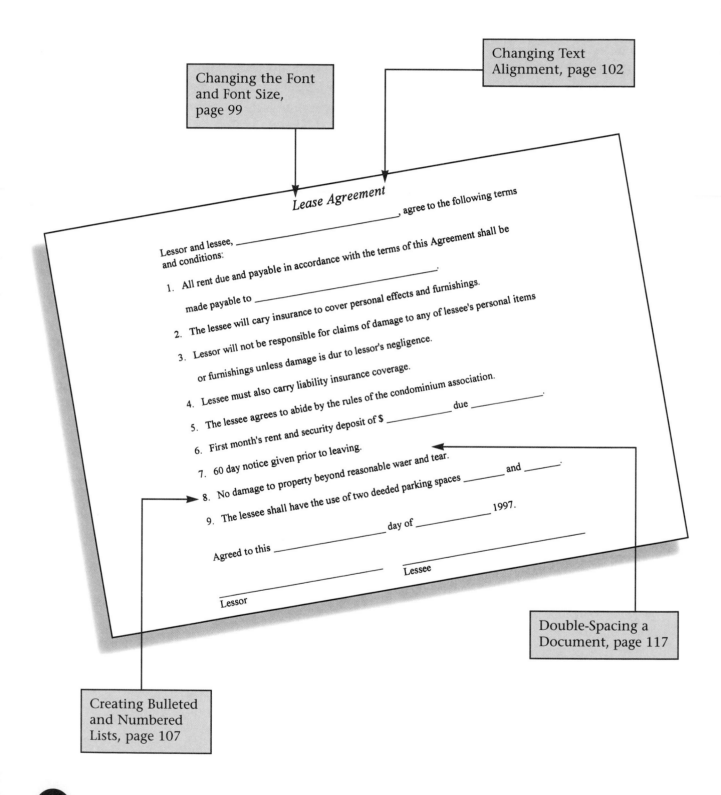

Changing the Font and Font Size, page 99

Changing Text Alignment, page 102

Lease Agreement

Lessor and lessee, _____, agree to the following terms and conditions:

1. All rent due and payable in accordance with the terms of this Agreement shall be made payable to _____.

2. The lessee will cary insurance to cover personal effects and furnishings.

3. Lessor will not be responsible for claims of damage to any of lessee's personal items or furnishings unless damage is dur to lessor's negligence.

4. Lessee must also carry liability insurance coverage.

5. The lessee agrees to abide by the rules of the condominium association.

6. First month's rent and security deposit of $ _____ due _____.

7. 60 day notice given prior to leaving.

8. No damage to property beyond reasonable waer and tear.

9. The lessee shall have the use of two deeded parking spaces _____ and _____.

Agreed to this _____ day of _____ 1997.

_____
Lessee

_____
Lessor

Double-Spacing a Document, page 117

Creating Bulleted and Numbered Lists, page 107

Create a Contract

1 The heading is set in Times New Roman, 16 point type, boldface, and centered. See these tasks:

2 The contract's body text is Times New Roman, 12 point type. A numbered list makes up the majority of the text. The document is also double-spaced. See these tasks:

3 Use the underscore to create the blank lines. Press and hold the underscore key while presing the Spacebar on the keyboard until the desired line length is reached.

4 Save and print the contract. See these tasks on saving and printing:

Using a Wizard,
page 88

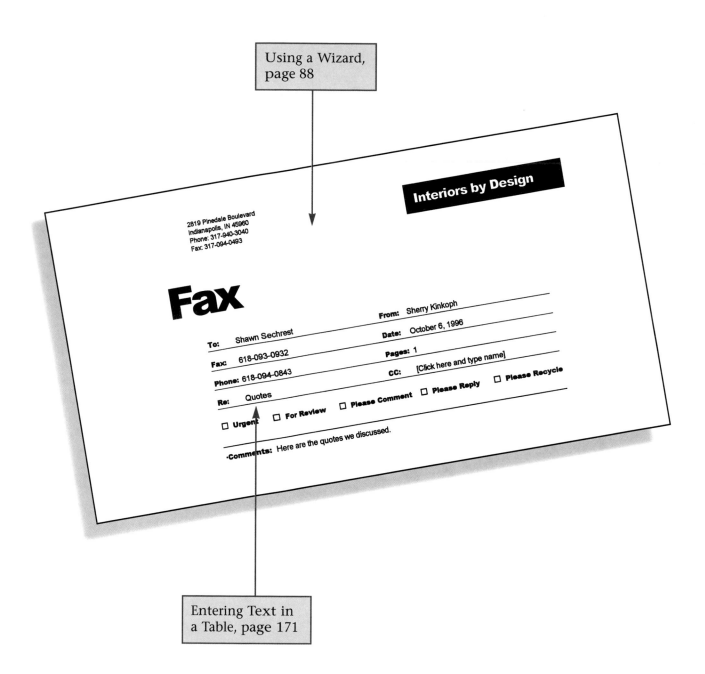

Interiors by Design

2819 Pinedale Boulevard
Indianapolis, IN 45960
Phone: 317-940-3040
Fax: 317-094-0493

Fax

		From: Sherry Kinkoph	
To: Shawn Sechrest		**Date:** October 6, 1996	
Fax: 618-093-0932		**Pages:** 1	
Phone: 618-094-0843		**CC:** [Click here and type name]	
Re: Quotes			

☐ **Urgent**   ☐ **For Review**   ☐ **Please Comment**   ☐ **Please Reply**   ☐ **Please Recycle**

·Comments: Here are the quotes we discussed.

Entering Text in
a Table, page 171

Create a Fax Cover Sheet

1 Use the Fax Wizard to create the fax cover sheet. Follow the instructions in each wizard dialog box. In this example, the fax cover sheet is portrait orientation and uses the Professional style. See this task:

Using a Wizard   *TASK 26, p. 88*

2 The fax cover sheet is in a table. If you want to add any text to the table, see this task for help:

Entering Text in a Table   *TASK 49, p. 171*

3 Save and print the fax cover sheet. See these tasks on saving and printing:

Saving a Document   *TASK 20, p. 72*

Printing the Document   *TASK 57, p. 196*

Index

Symbols

Index

Index

Index

Complete and Return this Card for a *FREE* Computer Book Catalog

Thank you for purchasing this book! You have purchased a superior computer book written expressly for your needs. To continue to provide the kind of up-to-date, pertinent coverage you've come to expect from us, we need to hear from you. Please take a minute to complete and return this self-addressed, postage-paid form. In return, we'll send you a free catalog of all our computer books on topics ranging from word processing to programming and the internet.

Mr. ☐   Mrs. ☐   Ms. ☐   Dr. ☐

Name (first) ☐☐☐☐☐☐☐☐☐☐☐☐   (M.I.) ☐   (last) ☐☐☐☐☐☐☐☐☐☐☐☐☐☐☐

Address ☐☐☐☐☐☐☐☐☐☐☐☐☐☐☐☐☐☐☐☐☐☐☐☐☐☐☐☐☐

☐☐☐☐☐☐☐☐☐☐☐☐☐☐☐☐☐☐☐☐☐☐☐☐☐☐☐☐☐

City ☐☐☐☐☐☐☐☐☐☐☐   State ☐☐   Zip ☐☐☐☐☐ ☐☐☐☐

Phone ☐☐☐ ☐☐☐ ☐☐☐☐   Fax ☐☐☐ ☐☐☐ ☐☐☐☐

Company Name ☐☐☐☐☐☐☐☐☐☐☐☐☐☐☐☐☐☐☐☐☐☐☐☐☐

E-mail address ☐☐☐☐☐☐☐☐☐☐☐☐☐☐☐☐☐☐☐☐☐☐☐☐☐

1. Please check at least (3) influencing factors for purchasing this book.

Front or back cover information on book .... ☐
Special approach to the content .... ☐
Completeness of content .... ☐
Author's reputation .... ☐
Publisher's reputation .... ☐
Book cover design or layout .... ☐
Index or table of contents of book .... ☐
Price of book .... ☐
Special effects, graphics, illustrations .... ☐
Other (Please specify): _____ ☐

2. How did you first learn about this book?

Saw in Macmillan Computer Publishing catalog .... ☐
Recommended by store personnel .... ☐
Saw the book on bookshelf at store .... ☐
Recommended by a friend .... ☐
Received advertisement in the mail .... ☐
Saw an advertisement in: _____ ☐
Read book review in: _____ ☐
Other (Please specify): _____ ☐

3. How many computer books have you purchased in the last six months?

This book only .... ☐   3 to 5 books .... ☐
2 books .... ☐   More than 5 .... ☐

4. Where did you purchase this book?

Bookstore .... ☐
Computer Store .... ☐
Consumer Electronics Store .... ☐
Department Store .... ☐
Office Club .... ☐
Warehouse Club .... ☐
Mail Order .... ☐
Direct from Publisher .... ☐
Internet site .... ☐
Other (Please specify): _____ ☐

5. How long have you been using a computer?

☐ Less than 6 months   ☐ 6 months to a year
☐ 1 to 3 years   ☐ More than 3 years

6. What is your level of experience with personal computers and with the subject of this book?

	With PCs	With subject of book
New	☐	☐
Casual	☐	☐
Accomplished	☐	☐
Expert	☐	☐

Source Code ISBN: 0-7897-1024-2

7. Which of the following best describes your job title?

Administrative Assistant .... ☐
Coordinator .... ☐
Manager/Supervisor .... ☐
Director .... ☐
Vice President .... ☐
President/CEO/COO .... ☐
Lawyer/Doctor/Medical Professional .... ☐
Teacher/Educator/Trainer .... ☐
Engineer/Technician .... ☐
Consultant .... ☐
Not employed/Student/Retired .... ☐
Other (Please specify): _____ ☐

8. Which of the following best describes the area of the company your job title falls under?

Accounting .... ☐
Engineering .... ☐
Manufacturing .... ☐
Operations .... ☐
Marketing .... ☐
Sales .... ☐
Other (Please specify): _____ ☐

Comments: _____
_____
_____

9. What is your age?

Under 20 .... ☐
21-29 .... ☐
30-39 .... ☐
40-49 .... ☐
50-59 .... ☐
60-over .... ☐

10. Are you:

Male .... ☐
Female .... ☐

11. Which computer publications do you read regularly? (Please list)

_____
_____
_____
_____
_____
_____
_____
_____
_____
_____

Fold here and scotch-tape to mail.